Bettering Humanomics

Bettering Humanomics

*A New, and Old, Approach
to Economic Science*

DEIRDRE NANSEN MCCLOSKEY

THE UNIVERSITY OF CHICAGO PRESS   CHICAGO AND LONDON

The University of Chicago Press, Chicago 60637
The University of Chicago Press, Ltd., London
© 2021 by The University of Chicago
All rights reserved. No part of this book may be used or reproduced in any manner
whatsoever without written permission, except in the case of brief quotations in critical
articles and reviews. For more information, contact the University of Chicago Press,
1427 E. 60th St., Chicago, IL 60637.
Published 2021
Printed in the United States of America

30 29 28 27 26 25 24 23 22 21   1 2 3 4 5

ISBN-13: 978-0-226-76592-1 (cloth)
ISBN-13: 978-0-226-76608-9 (e-book)
DOI: https://doi.org/10.7208/chicago/9780226766089.001.0001

Chapter 5 originally published as "One More Step: An Agreeable Reply to Whaples"
in *Historically Speaking* 11, no. 2 (2010): 22–23. © 2010 The Historical Society. Reprinted
with the permission of Johns Hopkins University Press.

Library of Congress Cataloging-in-Publication Data

Names: McCloskey, Deirdre N., author.
Title: Bettering humanomics : a new, and old, approach to economic science /
    Deirdre Nansen McCloskey.
Description: Chicago : University of Chicago Press, 2021. | Includes bibliographical
    references and index.
Identifiers: LCCN 2020048862 | ISBN 9780226765921 (cloth) | ISBN 9780226766089 (e-book)
Subjects: LCSH: Economics—Philosophy. | Economics—Moral and ethical aspects. |
    Economics—Sociological aspects.
Classification: LCC HB72.M329 2021 | DDC 330—dc23
LC record available at https://lccn.loc.gov/2020048862

♾ This paper meets the requirements of ANSI/NISO z39.48-1992 (Permanence of Paper).

Contents

Preface

The elevator pitch is that to get a better economic science we need "humanomics," which uses broader yet still rigorous theorizing and broader yet more serious empiricism than at present. And we need, as ethical social scientists, to be rigorously modest.[1]

During the 1980s and 1990s, as a middle-aged professor of economics, I wrote three books on method, saying that economics, like other sciences—and like the rest of the life of a speaking species—has a "rhetoric." That is, economics uses metaphors (*The Rhetoric of Economics*, 1985), stories (*If You're So Smart*, 1990), and epistemologies (*Knowledge and Persuasion in Economics*, 1994b). The books urged economists to become aware of their rhetoric if they wanted a grown-up science.

I don't claim that the books had much effect on my beloved colleagues. The economists, orthodox or not, carried on, bless 'em, with a positivism, behaviorism, and neoinstitutionalism in happy ignorance of the metaphors, stories, and epistemologies they use daily in their science.

So now in two books, this one and its forthcoming critical companion, *Beyond Behaviorism, Positivism, and Neoinstitutionalism in Economics*, I go further, to the substantive object, so to speak, of economic science. The economy itself has a rhetoric. The trilogy of earlier books was by contrast about the form of economic science. (I say this to the [small] extent that an elderly emerita professor of economics, of history, of communications, and of English can believe that form and substance are strictly separable.)

A technical book with Stephen Ziliak in 2008, *The Cult of Statistical Significance*, straddles the form and substance more explicitly. Its theme has recently been echoed by the American Statistical Association. The original articulation was as old as statistical theory itself. But its echo has not yet reached economists. (Science is of course conservative, and should be. Perhaps, though, the economists stoutly ignoring the common sense of statistical practice are taking conservation of old habits a bit too far.)

The ethics of liberalism, born in the eighteenth century, is part of humanomics. Liberalism is a foundational discipline for all the modern sciences, natural or social or humanistic. It's not an accident that science has flourished most in the more liberal societies, from ancient Athens to the modern Untied States. Good science—good social science most obviously—is made by good, honest, open-minded, liberal people, or else it is likely to break bad. Such a conclusion was sketched back in 1994 in *Knowledge and Persuasion in Economics*, and I finally got the politics of it more or less straight, I suppose, a quarter of a century later in *Why Liberalism Works* (2019). (I am not the swiftest of thinkers.) Clearly a bad, illiberal social engineering enables the tyrant to push people around. It breaks bad in every way. Therefore I argue in the other book of the present pair that Northian neoinstitutionalism, like the other antiethical, positivist, neobehaviorist, and illiberal movements over the past decades in economics, doesn't fit the bill for an ethical and persuasive economics for a free people.

Much of what I say here began as responses to invitations to sound off. "Responding," understand, is not merely irritated disputation or somehow impolite. It's the only alternative to a frozen and unproductive hierarchy in science of the sort that prevented for fifty years American geologists from believing in the movement of continents, prevented for thirty years Mayanists from decoding glyphs, and prevented for twenty years economists from challenging Keynesianism. Responding is what should be done by scientists—or by citizens or lawyers or marriage partners—every time, as amiably as they can manage. "What's your thought? Oh, I see. Hmm. Well, dear, here's my considered, and loving, response to your logic and your evidence, your feelings and your dignity. Maybe we can make your own thought better—certainly mine, for I readily admit that mine may be mistaken. Let's look into it. You come too." It's the human conversation of a good science, and it is why groups of loving friends in science and scholarship can criticize each other so productively. So, as you can see still more in the other book of the pair, I went to it with a will. (You're welcome.)

We should all try to follow the motto expressed by the philosopher Amélie Oksenberg Rorty, who wrote in 1983 that what is crucial is "our ability to engage in continuous conversation, testing one another, discovering our hidden pre-suppositions, changing our minds because we have listened to the voices of our fellows. Lunatics also change their minds, but their minds change with the tides of the moon and not because they have listened, really listened, to their friends' questions and objections."[2] Listening, really listening is the "hermeneutic" element in the triad of hermeneutic, rhetorical, and substantive/philosophical criticism.[3] The triad is how science advances, really advances, whether on little matters such as an econometric β coefficient or on world-shaping matters such as the big claims by Newton or Darwin or Marx or Keynes. The procedure is to listen, discovering the form of the argument, then use rhetorical and philosophical discernment to find out what's mistaken in the earlier science. Fix it. In 1867 the subtitle of Marx's *Capital* was *A Critique of Political Economy*. That's the scientific spirit.

The discoveries I have made by responding critically, yet as amiably as I could manage, are two:

1. There seems to be emerging a new and I think more serious and sensible way of doing economic science—quantitatively serious, philosophically serious, historically serious, and ethically serious, too, as I argue in this volume. The economist Bart Wilson and a few others nowadays call it the "humanomics," as in the title here.[4]

2. But, I argue in the other volume, neoinstitutionalism, from Douglass North and Daron Acemoglu and many other economists and political scientists, is not the way forward. Scientifically speaking, its factual claims, like those of the other recent neobehaviorist fashions, such as neuroeconomics and behavioral finance and happiness studies, are dubious—or, at best, questionably founded and argued. The neoinstitutionalists, like the others, do not listen, really listen, to the evidence of humans, or to their friends' scientific questions and objections. Substantively, they treat creative adults like a flock of little children, terrible twos, to whom we need not listen. We need, they say, merely to "observe their behavior," omitting for some reason linguistic behavior. And then we record the behavior in questionable metrics. The children-citizens will be pushed around with "incentives," beloved of Samuelsonian economists and econowannabes. From a great height of fatherly expertise in discerning and designing Max U institutions, the neoinstitutionalist looks down with contempt on the merely human actions and interactions of free adults.

So also, I say, do the other neobehaviorist fashions that stand against humanomics: a behavioral economics claiming that cognitively we are all of us little children; field experiments in economics performed pointlessly and often unethically on actual little children; a neuroeconomics hitching the little children up to electrodes, detecting a brain but not a mind; a happyism of meaningless metrics pleasing only to the tyrant of Bhutan; and, for the past century or so, reaching a climax recently, an economic engineering emanating from Washington or London or Brussels adding more and more "policies" to domineer over the silly little children—for their own good, you see. The US federal government has in place now over a million regulations. One million. The Democrats say, "Add more bureaucrats domineering over prescription drugs instead of permitting adult Americans to buy them freely abroad." The Republicans say, "Add more police domineering over northeast Baltimore instead of permitting adult Baltimoreans to consume what they want and to find employment at a wage that businesses are willing to pay."

All the neobehaviorist fashions go in the wrong direction, adopting an implausible and illiberal hypothesis that economic daddy knows best, treating grown-up people as less than fully dignified.[5] And the vaunted empiricism of neobehaviorism in all its forms turns out to be startlingly hollow. To overcome the illiberalism and fill up the hollows, we need a better economics, a bettering humanomics, an economics with the humans left in. Smith, Wicksteed, Hirschman, Klamer, Wilson.

Whether or not you are an academic economist, you should care about the humanomical future and the recent behaviorist past of the field. Madmen in authority, it has been said, who hear voices in the air, are distilling their frenzy from some academic scribbler a few years back. The distilled products of behaviorism are the policies of the Politburo, the Council of the European Union, the Federal Reserve Bank, the Chinese Communist Party, the US Treasury, the IMF, the World Bank, the federal and state and local governments, Bernie Sanders, Joseph Stiglitz, Paul Krugman, Marianna Mazzucato, and the very idea that there should be proliferating policies and regulations devised by omnicompetent masters to govern the pathetic little lives of stupid, irrational little children. You, for example, dearie. You should care if such a distillation will demean and then kill you.

Still, the main implied reader of the books is a professional economist or a fellow traveler among political scientists, sociologists, law professors, and philosophers. I've been an economist and economic historian most of my life, and I love and admire economics and economists and economic historians. Mostly. Paul Samuelson and Milton Friedman, Geoff Harcourt and Harry Johnson, Bob Fogel and Albert Hirschman, Harold Demsetz and Joan Robinson, Friedrich Hayek and Bob Heilbroner. Hurrah for the idea of opportunity cost, of supply and demand, of general equilibrium, of entry and exit, with all their mathematical and statistical expressions. Three cheers for the accounting of national income and the wheel of wealth, especially in its historical implementations. The Lord's blessing on cooperation and competition, their analysis and their analysts. Yes, I said, yes I will yes.

But if the distillation is not to demean and then kill you and me and pretty much everyone else from Boston to Beijing, we economists need to rethink the recipe, devising a humanomics that nonetheless does not throw away what's known from good old economic science. (A careless throwing away typifies proposals for this or that "new" economics, from many Marxists and institutionalists down to all the Modern Monetary Theorists and up to loony protectionists in foreign trade and loony anti-immigrants in foreign migration led by Peter Navarro and Steven Miller under Trump.) In brief, serious economists need a serious rethinking of their scientism, their sneering dismissal of ethics, their illiberalism even while claiming the honorable title of liberal, their "cargo-cult" pretense of quantification, and their accompanying scorn for most of human knowledge and behavior.

"Cargo-cult" may need explanation. It's the label the physicist Richard Feynman assigned to projects having the external look of science but that are actually make-believe.[6] His metaphor refers to the highlanders of New Guinea after World War II, who set up coconut-shell lamps and runway-like clearings in the cultish hope that the big wartime planes with their enriching cargo would come back. The planes didn't actually come back. Similarly, much of what passes for high-level evidence in economics *looks* like quantification, or at any rate matrix algebra, but doesn't relevantly quantify or yield actual truths about the work of the world. And much of what passes for high-level theorizing in economics *looks* like insight into the world and its work, but doesn't yield that, either.

The "sneering dismissal of ethics . . . and their accompanying scorn for most of human knowledge," does not need much explanation. It's positivism, and is the main obstacle to a bettering humanomics. You see it in action daily. The very word *science* is commonly used as a club to beat people with, in ignorance of the actual philosophy, sociology, and history of science since Kuhn and in ignorance that in all languages except recent English, the word *science* means "systematic study," and not only of the physical world. The ignoramuses—among them many economic scientists—proceed to ignore ethics and to exclude a priori other ways of knowing.

A future economics should on the contrary use the available scientific logic and evidence, all of it—experimental, simulative, introspective, questionnaire, graphical, categorical, statistical, literary, historical, psychological, sociological, political, aesthetic, ethical. To deploy an old joke, the economist drunk on his specialized distillation should stop assuming that his house keys, which he lost out in the dark, have mysteriously shown up under the lamppost, where, he explains, the light is better. The economist should become seriously quantitative and seriously *qualitative*, too, practicing an entire human science. Get the numbers right *and* the categories. No more cargo cults, dears. Get serious ethically. Search for all the scientifically relevant knowledge out in the dark, where much of it is to be found, not exclusively under the lamppost.

PART I
The Proposal

CHAPTER ONE

Humanomics and Liberty Promise Better Economic Science

I offer here, in the first of this pair of books, a prospect, with examples in some detail, for that better and bettering humanomics. The word names an economic science that accepts (with commonsense repairs) the models and mathematics and statistics and experiments and the like of the orthodoxy circa 2021 but then adds the immense amount we can learn about human action in the economy from the myriad forms of human speech if we will but listen, really listen—the news on the Rialto, the rhetoric of the chat rooms in controlled experiments, the sober testimony of businesspeople at Rotary meetings, the gossip of the *Kaffeeklatsch*, the findings of interspecies experiments, the results of value alignment in AI, the politics on the stump and in the cloakroom, the ethical and epistemological ruminations about suitable categories (national income, to be sure, but which definition of the nation, or of income?), the stories of historians, the reflections of theologians, the introspections of poets and philosophers, the surveys of public opinion, the wisdom of the visual arts and of songs, films, plays, novels, poems, operas, the Grand Ole Opry. And, concerning all of this human speaking, a humanomics marshals, too, the reflection *about* the art and speech, what are called in America "the humanities" and in Britain "arts subjects," the enormous, ramifying project since ancient times of looking back critically on human thinking and speaking and their results in human action. In short, we economists should use all the evidence we can get our hands on. If we don't, we aren't being serious scientists but mere drunks of scientism, or New Guinea highlanders.

As put by the Chinese psychologist and economic thinker Ning Wang and the 1991 Nobelist Ronald Coase, a pioneer of humanomics before the letter, "The stupendous loss in the depth and richness of human nature is a noticeable part of the price we have paid in transforming economics from a moral science of man creating wealth to a cold logic of choice in resource allocation. No longer a study of man as he is, modern economics has lost its anchor and drifted away from economic reality. As a result, economists are hard pressed to say much that is coherent and insightful, although their counsel is badly needed in this time of crisis and uncertainty."[1]

In *Round the Bend* (1951) the Australian novelist Nevil Shute (most famous for *On the Beach* [1957], made in 1959 into a poignant film starring Gregory Peck) told of the owner of an air-transport company reflecting on his business after the death of his brilliant chief engineer Constantien (he was called Connie, and was a religious man):

> I was lonely and troubled, and at first there didn't seem to be much point in going on with anything; I was very tired, and I didn't know what to do. I thought of selling out my business, to Airservice, perhaps. . . . But after a time I got settled down, and then it seemed to me that it would be a better thing to carry on the business and run it in the way that Connie liked, so that in a materialistic world my air line should be an example running through Asia to show that men can keep the aircraft safe by serving God in Connie's way, and yet keep on the black side of the ledger. I'd go so far as to say, from my experience, that only by serving God in this way can you keep out of the red.[2]

Shute is pointing to a human characteristic, our need for a transcendent purpose, even in business, and our need for the guidance of love, even in business. It's just the way nonsociopathic humans are, in addition to their pursuit of materialistic profit. The pursuit of profit, after all, is shared with all of life, from bacteria and moss through our cousins the great apes. It's not at all especially human. A *human* science about "the ordinary business of life" (as Alfred Marshall a long time ago defined economics) needs to acknowledge such nonprofit purposes as much as it acknowledges balance sheets. It doesn't give up what we learned from Adam Smith or Marshall or Keynes or Samuelson. An Adam Smithian science would combine what the first editor of the *Economist*, Walter Bagehot, called in his exposition of the British constitution the "efficient" and the "dignified," the quotidian and the transcendent, the means and the ends. Both. Thus, humanomics.

Economists routinely defend their sneering dismissal of ethics and their accompanying scorn for most of human knowledge by appealing to specialization. "Ah, you see, economics itself recommends specialization. Shoemaker, stick to your last." But they don't then complete the economics. Piling up specialized products in the backyard is pointless if one does not trade them. Specialization, *and then trade*, is what economics since Adam Smith recommends. An economist dismissing the transcendent purposes of economic actors, ignoring their talk, and treating them like ants to be observed, isn't trading with other human knowledge.

We are, you will have noticed, humans. A big part of our human behavior is thinking and talking about human action, not merely solipsistic and thoughtless *re*action to, say, a budget constraint. Human action (a technical term in the Austrian economics of Mises and Hayek and Lachmann and Kirzner and Lavoie and Boettke) is the exercise of free will, so typical of humans. It is in fact the free will about which theologians argue. Humanomics therefore goes beyond the artificially narrowed evidence of a silent, solitary, reactive, positivistic, predestined, observational behaviorism.

Behaviorism has ruled economics and many other fields of the human sciences since the 1930s, but without much philosophical reflection about what a speaking species does. In opposing for the human species such a behaviorism, the entomologist E. O. Wilson, when asked about a top-down, behaviorist idea for treating humans like ants, such as in thoroughgoing Marxism, said, "Karl Marx was right, socialism works, it is just that he had the wrong species."[3] The Austrian American economist and early student of the rhetoric of economics, Fritz Machlup, pointedly asked what physics would look like if atoms could . . . wait for it . . . talk.[4] For a science of talking humans, it is still a highly relevant question.

The word *humanomics* was coined around 2010, I have noted, by the astonishing experimental economist Bart Wilson, who with the Nobelist Vernon Smith wrote in 2019 *Humanomics: Moral Sentiments and the Wealth of Nations for the Twenty-First Century*. Then in 2020 Wilson, who is also professor of law, wrote a humanomical study of the uniquely human habit of alienable property in a book called *The Property Species: How Humans Make Things "Mine," How "Mine" Makes Us Human*. For many years Wilson has taught with Jan Osborn (a colleague from the Department of English at Chapman University in California) a freshman course introducing economics through such texts as an English translation of Goethe's *Faust*.

Yes, you heard that right, *Faust*. Early in the epic, for instance, the misled Doctor Faust articulates a complaint that illuminatingly violates the no-free-lunch postulate of economics or its related twenty-shilling-note theorem. The theorem is that routine learning, picking up twenty-shilling notes that might perhaps have fallen on the roadside, earns merely routine profits:

> Proof. Axiom: humans are acquisitive. Fact: they eagerly pick up twenty-shilling notes lying on the roadside. Fact: there are plenty of such humans entering most roads. And there are often no powerful ethical prohibitions, or no thugs from the mafia or the government, preventing the entry of the pickers-up. Conclusion: Not many twenty-shilling notes lie around for Faust to pick up on the basis of routine knowledge. ∎

The Doctor whines, "I have neither money nor treasures. / Nor worldly honors of earthly pleasures."[5] Routine learning, he is complaining, has not resulted in a free lunch of supernormal profits. It is a childish and antieconomic complaint, implied daily in the chatter of "technical analysts" on CNBC. He therefore turns to magic, or chartist financial advisers, or econometricians, "That I might see what secret force / Hides in the world."[6] And finally in vexation he turns to Mephistopheles.

Humanomics learns, then, from *Faust* as from covered interest arbitrage. The full range of such an approach will become evident. Philosophers note that one sort of definition of a term is "ostensive" (Latin *ostendere*, to show). You can show what is meant by the word *chair* by showing a dozen of them in varied designs, from Windsor to Eames. This book provides an ostensive definition of humanomics.

But recently it hit me that over the past fifteen years I've provided such an ostensive definition of humanomics without realizing it—speaking prose without realizing it—in the trilogy on the economics and history of the Bourgeois Era (2006, 2010, 2016), and in the popular version written with Art Carden, *Leave Me Alone and I'll Make You Rich: How the Bourgeois Deal Enriched the World* (2020), and in the political book I've mentioned, *Why Liberalism Works* (2019). Then it hit me, too, in rereading the short critical and responsive pieces I've been writing all my academic career on history, economics, and liberalism, gathered now under the rubric of *Impromptus* in three volumes, that I've been reaching for a humanomics in a confused way since the 1960s. And—now more self-consciously—I propose later to do it again, in a planned book on English agricultural history, *The Prudent and Faithful Peasant: An Essay in Historical Humanomics*, and even, God willing, in a theological book, *God in Mammon: Episcopalian Sermons*. Crazy.

Yet even so I am embarrassingly late to the party. Much earlier works by wiser economists than I, such as Albert Hirschman and Arjo Klamer, back to the blessed Adam Smith himself, anticipated humanomics many decades, if not centuries, before I finally and fully realized it. They show an economics going beyond behaviorism to establish a real, non–cargo-cult science.

* * *

So the humanomics exhibited in this book of the pair is an extended example of getting beyond the orthodoxy—the neoinstitutionalism and other little-child behaviorisms criticized in the other book. The pair together propose instead that we economists grow up and get seriously modest about the logic and evidence of a human science, embracing the liberty and the creativity of adults.

Economic logic itself contradicts social engineering in its varied forms. If the social engineers were so smart, as I noted long ago in studying the rhetoric of storytelling in economics, why aren't they rich?[7] Industrial policy, anyone? It's a fair question to ask of any expert proposing to run your life with helpful suggestions or with coerced policies based on an alleged ability to predict the future. Supernormal profit, as Dr. Faust understood, is a strict implication of a supposed ability to predict and control. Yet we can't predict and control, not profitably, not in a creative economy. Name the economist who predicted the internet or containerization or the Green Revolution or the automobile or the modern university or the steam engine. If you think you can name one, I'll doubt it until you show me her bank account. "If thou find'st one, let me know, / Such a pilgrimage were sweet; / Yet do not, I would not go, / Though at next door we might meet." Growing up requires an expanded but modest humanistic science that analyzes the creativity of human action in retrospect and accepts in prospect the epistemological limits on ant-like prediction and control. It's the humanities in humanomics.

The recommendation to take the humanities seriously in economics, understand, is not an attack on mathematics. I side with Léon Walras, who wrote in 1874, "As for those economists who do not know any mathematics, who do not know what is meant by mathematics and yet have taken the stand that mathematics cannot possibly serve to elucidate economic principles, let them go their way repeating that 'human liberty will *never* allow itself to be cast into equations' or that 'mathematics ignores frictions which are *everything* in social science."[8] If you want my opinion (no extra charge), I think there should be *more* mathematics and statistics in economics, not less—though I have long argued that many of the present tools along such lines constitute a cargo cult. We should do more scientifically relevant mathematics and statistics, not less, and at a much higher level than we do now. We should do simulations and error bounds, Bayesian analysis and functional approximations, learned from engineering and physics, with evolutionary mathematics learned from biology, instead of grinding away at pointless existence theorems, on/off, learned from the Department of Mathematics, and pointless *t*-tests, on/off, learned from a Fisherian, anti-Bayesian Department of Statistics.[9] And we should get beyond the Samuelsonian commandment that all models have to consist of the adventures of a sociopath named Max U.

The lesson of humanomics, in short, is that modesty in the face of creativity by free adults is in order. No more human masters. God and nature alone master us. In the way Rachel Carson argued about silent springs in 1963, Jane Jacobs in 1984 argued about vibrant cities: "Germane correction depends on fostering creativity in whatever forms it happens to appear in a given city at a given time. It is impossible to know in advance."[10] DDT looked like a miracle treatment, and asbestos looked like a miracle material, and econometrics looked like a miracle tool of economic engineering until they didn't. Robert Moses's takings by eminent domain in New York City looked brilliant until they didn't. Brilliant miracles are not routinely achievable by central plan. The production function, if it is imagined to be about masterful causes rather than a modest retrospective accounting (as Moses Abramowitz wisely put it, "a measure of our ignorance"), is cargo-cult science. I myself practiced it for decades, *mea maxima culpa*. We humans live in economies the way we live in cities and in language and in art and in cookery and in the natural environment. Attempts at overmastering by central planning usually do not work. We should restrain therefore the impulse for a masterful prediction and control, an impulse theorized in Auguste Comte's constructivist rubric two centuries ago *savoir pour pouvoir*. As it was put by the philosopher Yogi Berra (and, it turns out, the physicist Niels Bohr), in the face of human creativity, or of quantum mechanics, prediction is difficult, especially about the future. So, therefore, is control.

Stop it. Then get serious about a richly descriptive yet ethically restrained human science of economic life. Humanomics.

CHAPTER TWO

Adam Smith Practiced Humanomics, and So Should We

L et's start therefore where it started, with that blessed Adam Smith. A worrying feature of economic science as now practiced is that it ignores language in the economy. To put it another way, economics has ignored the humanities, such as philosophy and literature, theology and history, and the related social sciences, too, such as cultural anthropology and qualitative sociology—that is, it has ignored the study of human meaning. Yet Adam Smith, may his tribe increase, spoke often of "the faculty of speech" and *did* consider meaning in all his writings. "The offering of a shilling," he wrote (or, rather, said, because the source is notes by students on his lectures), "which to us appears to have so plain and simple a meaning, is in reality offering an argument to persuade one to do so and so as it is for his interest."[1]

People do not merely silently offer shillings and silently hand over haircuts. People are not, as Samuelsonian economics supposes, vending machines. They talk, or as the economist and pioneer of humanomics Arjo Klamer puts it (in 2011, among other of his works back to his first book in 1983), they converse. And in conversing they open each other to modifications of the price, as it may be. Anyway, by conversation they establish, as we say, the "going" price—which is how the paradoxes of continuous traders and so forth in Arrow-Debreu formulations are solved in practice and why experimental markets work so amazingly well despite appearing not to correspond with the Arrow-Debreu conditions even approximately.[2] The other Smith I have mentioned—Vernon—noted that "the principal findings of experimental economics are that impersonal exchange in markets converges in repeated interaction to the equilibrium states implied by economic theory, under information conditions far weaker than specified in the theory. In personal, social, and economic exchange, as studied in two-person games, cooperation exceeds the prediction of traditional game theory."[3] To put it mildly.

Market participants, Adam Smith the student of rhetoric continues, "in this manner . . . acquire a certain dexterity and address in managing their affairs, or in other words in managing of men [and of women, s.v.p., my dear Adam]; and this is altogether the practice of every man in the most ordinary affairs."[4] It is the practice of address, for example, in the ordinary affairs of academic economics itself (as I argued during the 1980s and 1990s in books on the rhetoric of economics). And certainly a rhetoric figures largely in the ordinary affairs of the economy itself, as I later realized (calculating it with Arjo Klamer and then in the Bourgeois Era trilogy applying it to the ethics and history of the modern world). Old Adam knew it two and a half centuries before I did: "In this manner everyone is practicing oratory on others through the whole of his life."[5]

Adam Smith's first book, *The Theory of Moral Sentiments* (1759; sixth edition 1790, the year of his death), the one he loved the best, which most economists (like me until about 1990) have never heard of, is about how we converse in public or in the councils of our hearts about ethics, especially about the virtue of temperance. And even in his other book, concerning the virtue of prudence, which economists *have* heard of but mostly have not actually read (that, too, describes your reporter until about 1990), he writes, "whether this propensity [to truck and barter] be one of those original principles in human nature, of which no further account can be given; or whether, as seems more probable, it be the necessary consequence of the faculties of reason [thus Samuelsonian economics] *and speech* [thus a Smithian humanomics], it belongs not to our present subject to inquire."[6] Alas. One wishes that he had pushed the inquiry further on that score. In the *Lectures on Jurisprudence* he had said (as the editors observe about the passage just quoted from *The Wealth of Nations*), "the real foundation of [the division of labor] is that principle to persuade which so much prevails in human nature."[7]

Smith's followers, however, gradually set aside language and persuasion and meaning in favor of what they fancied was a machinery predictable from the outside of human liberty. Until the 1930s the setting aside was gentle and nondogmatic, allowing for occasional intrusions of human meaning, such as Keynes on animal spirits or Dennis Robertson on economized love.[8] But in the shadow of early twentieth-century positivism and

under the influence of Lionel Robbins, Paul Samuelson, and Milton Friedman (and then Richard Lipsey and Michael Jensen and Gary Becker and
many others), the study of the economy was reduced strictly to "behavior" (ignoring, illogically, most *linguistic* behavior; in this, too, the school
of Vernon Smith and Bart Wilson and others has gone beyond the predictions of traditional game theory by *listening* to the cooperating and com-
peting experimental subjects practicing oratory on others).

But what, an economist would reply, of studies by George Stigler
(1961) and Jacob Marschak (1968) and George Akerlof (1970) and many
others since the 1960s on the transmittal of information? Yes, good: information is often linguistically transmitted. Surely one of the main de-
velopments in economics since the 1960s has been the acknowledgment
of information and signaling. Fine. Got it. But the sort of language that
can be treated by routine formulations of marginal benefit and marginal
cost—which is the Procrustean bed on which all recent studies of language in the economy have so far been forced to lie, such as in a book
by Ariel Rubinstein in 2000—is *merely* the transmittal of information or
commands: "I offer $4.15 for a bushel of corn"; "I accept your offer"; "No
deal." It is the language of vending machines. The trouble is that a large
portion of talk in the economy, as Adam and Vernon Smith have said, is
not merely informing or commanding but persuading by sweet or not-so-
sweet talk: "Your price is absurdly high"; "We need to work together if
our company is to succeed"; "I have a brilliant idea for making cooling
fans for automobiles, and you should invest in it"; "The new iPhone is
lovely"; "Intellectual products should not be property, because they have
zero opportunity cost in use."

Does it matter? Does persuasive talk have economic significance? Yes.
Klamer and I showed, and I will show here in detail later, that on the
basis of occupational statistics for the United States about a quarter of
labor income in a modern economy is earned by sweet talk—not by lies
or trickery always but mainly by the honest persuasion that a manager
must exercise in a society of free workers or that a teacher must exercise
to persuade her students to read books or that a lawyer must exercise if a
society of laws is to be meaningful.

If language in the economy were merely "cheap talk," as the (well-
named) noncooperative game theorists put it, then ignoring it would not
matter, and its share of economic activity would drift toward zero. If we
were vending machines, no one would pay for persuasion. What would be
the point? You pay your money and you take your choice. An economic

agent would be no more valuable if she were a sweet rather than a sour conduit for transmitted bids and asks. The chattering character of people in markets and firms and households about their economic affairs would be like left-handedness or red hair—interesting maybe for some purposes, in the Department of English or in the hair salon, but irrelevant to the tough, macho, scientific matter of the economy.[9]

That, however, is not the case. Formal maximum-utility economics can-*not* explain sweet talk, and the sweet talk matters greatly. An early example in modern social science of such thinking—anticipated, to be sure, by thousands of years of literary explorations of the same point, such as most plays of Shakespeare—is the political scientist Edward Banfield's classic of 1958 about a village in southern Italy, *The Moral Basis of a Backward Society*: "In a society of amoral familists [as Banfield called them, from their treatment of the family as the only relevant moral object, as in *The Sopranos*], no one will further the interests of the community except as it is to his private advantage."[10] Banfield's is an impossibility theorem. Max U doesn't have to talk, unlike Klamer's or Hirschman's or Elinor Ostrom's conversationalists. Banfield's southern Italian merely follows the rules of a noncooperative game.

Yet the oldest and most obvious point in game theory, and in games, is that the rules of a game can be modified by conversation in agreed ways. Early in the history of chess a bishop could move only one space at a time. Then the rule was changed, and the bishop pin became possible. A long time ago my spouse and I played a game of Monopoly with dear Israeli American friends, Joel and Margalit Mokyr, visiting our home in Iowa City. The McCloskeys prided themselves on being pretty canny Monopoly players—exercising, for example, the one-order-up metarule of *always* building houses on a monopoly immediately, and especially on the orange New York Avenue triplet. But the Mokyrs outplayed us with ease because they were willing to play—within the loose framework of the official rules of the game—at the *second* order up, proposing side deals, such as for conditional exemptions from rent. "You sell me your New York Avenue card for $1,000 in Monopoly money and I will promise not to charge you rent if you land on its monopoly. But only two times." Sweet talk emerges willy-nilly, as the political scientist Elinor Ostrom and her economist colleagues such as Roy Gardner showed.[11] Indeed, experimental economics in the past few decades has shown repeatedly that allowing experimental subjects to establish relationships through conversation radically increases the degree of cooperation. Just let the kids talk and they suddenly cooperate. So in markets.

"The bonds of words are too weak," Hobbes declared, "to bridle men's ambitions, avarice, anger, and other passions, without the fear of some coercive power."[12] Oh, no, fierce Thomas, no. Words do sometimes bind the impartial spectator within the breast—and at the least they offer counsel, as in proverbs. So even economists could be shamed by taking an oath to do no harm and to seek truth earnestly.[13] Business works with verbally shaped trust in "good old trustworthy Max"—not with endless suspicion of nasty old Max U, the silent maximizer of utility in a noncooperative, Samuelsonian way, who cannot be trusted at all except to attempt his own sociopathic purpose.[14]

What made Donald Trump's business and political practices successful, to the small extent that in the end they were, was that he systematically defected from every element of the trust on which human cooperation is based. He never paid his subcontractors what he had promised; he always sued them if they complained. That businesspeople, and eventually the voters, were startled by and then became indignant at his behavior shows vividly how commonplace the opposite—honorable, decent behavior—actually is in human affairs shaped by language. Joe Biden.

Maximizing utility is not human meaning, as one can see in mothers and in suicide bombers. As one of the framers of behaviorist economics (an economics I disapprove of, though I approve of the man himself), Robert Frank, wisely put it, "When a man dies shortly after drinking the used crankcase oil from his car, we do not really explain anything by asserting that he must have had a powerful taste for crankcase oil."[15] The framing of bargaining depends on the stories people tell.[16] The language, the trust, the sweet talk, the conversations—all depend on ethical commitments beyond Max U's "I'm all right, Jack."

The literature bearing on the matter even in economics itself has recently become large, ranging from Klamer to Vernon Smith to Herbert Gintis. The Austrian economists such as Friedrich Hayek and Israel Kirzner recognized long ago the importance of discovery and other human action beyond a routine maximization in reaction to constraints. But even the Austrians mostly stopped short of grasping the role of language, a defect that their students and the students of their students, especially at George Mason University, are bent on overcoming. The late Don Lavoie of George Mason above all embarked on such a program, inspired by Ludwig Lachmann. Then Donald Boudreaux, Jack High, Karen Vaughn, Peter Boettke, Dan Klein, Lawrence White, Virgil Storr, and Emily Chamlee-Wright, among others, follow it. The New Austrians of GMU, and new Austrians elsewhere such as Mario Rizzo at New York University or Steven Horwitz at Ball State University or David Prychitko of Northern Michigan University, point out that real discoveries, such as that a separate condenser makes a steam engine more efficient or that treating the bourgeoisie with something other than contempt results in economic growth, arise as it were by accident—as Kirzner puts it in another chess metaphor, en passant. Real discoveries (Joel Mokyr calls them macroinventions) cannot be pursued methodically—or else they are known before they are known, a paradox.[17] Yet once a discovery is made by what Kirzner calls "alertness," it requires sweet talk to be brought to fruition. An idea is merely an idea until it has been brought into the conversation of humankind. And so the modern world has depended on sweet talk, the spring in the economic watch.

CHAPTER THREE

Economic History Illustrates the Problems with Nonhumanomics

A natural place where economic science can exercise a Smithian humanomics is economic history, that is, the study of the past of economies such as Scotland's or France's or China's. It's "natural" because we have in economic history an amazing technique for looking into the minds even of dead people, a technique that many in economics deny themselves, called . . . uh . . . reading. It is a form of listening, really listening to the people in the economy. We can know what is in the minds of the glorious dead. Remarkable. We do not need to settle merely for external measurements, such as blood flow to various parts of a living brain, as useful as they might be for certain narrow purposes. If minds and language, as against the merely physical and (partial) behavioral evidence also used for studying ants and chimps, matter for economic science, it's good to have such a mind-reading technique at hand and to use it. Economics, and especially historical economics, cannot live by behavior and blood flow alone.

The future of economics, therefore, may be discernable in the present of economic history and especially in its near-term promise. Unhappily, to be realistic, it is probable that economic historians will continue for the next decade or so to be dominated by a behavioral scientism, a cargo cult quite different from actual science.

I worry in economic history, for example, about "analytical narratives," which are popular with neoinstitutionalists of the Northian tendency. Certainly the contribution of economic history to economics consists in part of the narrativizing of economic behavior, a moving picture as against the more usual snapshot, as the economic historian and macroeconomist the late Richard Sutch so persuasively argued and showed.[1] The trouble is the lack of meaningful quantitative testing. Quantification doesn't happen much at all in historical neoinstitutionalism (for instances, see the other book of this pair). If the economic analysis is "consistent with" some little piece of economic history, all is said to be well. The procedure is a zombie form of logical positivism. What one would like to see is quantitative oomph such as in the economic histories by Jeffrey Williamson (What's the oomph in a general-equilibrium simulation?), or else the humanist's substitute for quantity, serious comparative histories such as in the economic histories of Alexander Gerschenkron (Does it work in Russia?).[2] Either or both would do.

No sensible person is against theory if it means economic ideas, even if only of a qualitative, classifying sort. It does not matter whether the economic idea comes dressed in mathematics or in diagrams or in words. The idea can be informational asymmetry. Signaling. Entry and exit. Computable general equilibrium. Property rights. Transaction costs. Good. But if all we have is an analytical narrative or a qualitative theorem, none actually tested in the world, even in the (largely empty) set of ones that can be, what do we have, scientifically speaking?

Ah, you will reply, but we *do* test, with econometrics. A scientistic historical economics has recently settled on econometrics as the only tool for testing.

No, we don't test with it, and no, it is not the right tool. Name the important economic fact since the Second World War that has been rejected or accepted by specifically *econometric* test (again, the other book gives details). Robert Fogel subtitled his study *Railroads and American Economic Growth* of 1964 *Essays in Econometric History*. But Fogel did not in fact use econometrics even by the primitive definition of 1964. He used simulation. About that same time the economist Rich Weisskoff and I served as (incompetent) graduate research assistants for John Meyer at Harvard, helping to edit his essays with Alfred Conrad for a book entitled *The Economics of Slavery: And Other Studies in Econometric History* (which also came out in 1964). Meyer and Conrad in fact used simulation and accounting and economic ideas with hardly a *t*-test in sight. One of Meyer's simulations, for example, was an input-output study of British growth in the late nineteenth century. (After a while I realized, being at the time a recovering input-output addict, that the technique was useless for explaining growth, especially beyond a single recovery in the business cycle. It was the beginning of a slow realization—I mean "slow" as in "four decades later"—expressed above in the introduction.[3] I realized that Leontief's input-output analysis and indeed Samuelson's production-function analysis can give a mechanical, post hoc account of routine activity, with today the same as yesterday, but do not identify the causes of the creative explosion that characterizes the modern world.)

The Conrad and Meyer book took its title from simulation and accounting about the profitability of US slavery. Nowhere did the book use econometrics, though Meyer was at the time a leading applied econometrician and Conrad had spent a year at Jan Tinbergen's famous shop in Rotterdam that had invented econometrics. There is nothing wrong, of course, with fitting hyperplanes to observational data. Some of my best friends are hyperplanes. What turns the innocuous method of looking at the data with multiple regressions into a cargo cult is the use of t-tests to select the important variables. It can't, although most economists, contrary as I have noted to the wisdom of the American Statistical Association, still think it can.

The usual training in quantitative methods in graduate school in economics is fully three terms of econometrics, such as I took (with Meyer in one course and Guy Orcutt, the pioneering simulator, for the rest). It gives no training in other empirical methods—such as simulation (by Meyer and Orcutt and Barbara Bergmann and a few others, and especially at the time in agricultural economics), archival research, experiment, surveys, graphing, national income accounting, serious introspection (after all, we are the very economic atoms). "Test, test, test," declares the econometrician David Hendry. The trouble is that such tests of "significance," which is what Hendry means, are bankrupt, as for example the theorist Kenneth Arrow noted in 1957. And now I say again (check it out, guys) the statisticians of the American Statistical Association have come to agree with Arrow.[4]

Let's get back to Smith, that great empiricist.

CHAPTER FOUR

An Economic Science Needs the Humanities

E nough, already, of reality. What do I *want* economic history and therefore economics to become? What are my hopeful predictions, in the short run admittedly unrealistic? In brief, I hope economic history continues to be the scientific part of economics and of history but gets even more scientific than it is now by expanding into humanomics.

Realize, though, as I have already briefly noted, that the word *science* is a big problem in English and has long misled economists and economic historians to try to imitate what they imagine goes on in physics. In all other languages, from French to Chinese and back, the local science word means merely "systematic inquiry" as distinct from, say, casual journalism or unsupported opinion. In German, for example, *Geisteswissenschaften*—which translates literally into English as a spooky-sounding "spirit sciences"—is the normal German word for the humanities. The Dutch speak of *kunstwetenschap*, "art science," which English speakers now would call "art history" or "theory of art" and place firmly in the humanities, arrayed against science—*only* in modern English. In Italy a proud mother of a twelve-year-old girl who is doing well at school speaks of *mia scienziata*, which sounds very strange in recent English: "my scientist."

In earlier English, *Wissenschaft* or *wetenschap* or *scienza* was what "science" also meant. Thus, Alexander Pope in 1711, *An Essay on Criticism* (lines 221–24): "While from the bounded level of our mind / Short views we take, nor see the lengths behind: / But more advanced, behold with strange surprise / New distant scenes of endless science rise."[1] He didn't mean an imitation of natural philosophy. Then in the mid-nineteenth century, as a result it seems of disputes over chairs of chemistry at Oxford and Cambridge, the word was specialized to the systematic study of the physical world. In the *Oxford English Dictionary* the new meaning, slowly adopted from the 1860s on (Alfred Marshall never did adopt it, but by the time of Keynes everyone had), was recorded as sense 5b—the dominant sense now, the lexicographers of Oxford inform us, in ordinary usage.

The usage of the last century and a half makes for endless, foolish disputes about "whether economics is a science" and gives natural scientists permission to issue haughty sneers about social *science*. (Feynman's joke about "cargo cults" that I have used was aimed, ignorantly, alas, at sociology.) Yet what would it matter to the practice if we decided that economics and economic history, and for that matter sociology, were *not* sciences? I suppose we social scientists would be expelled peremptorily from the National Science Foundation and the National Academy of Sciences, which would be sad and unprofitable. But would the banishment change the actual practice of economic or historical science? It might, but probably for the better.

In actual practice the sort of categorical qualia that occupy humanistic sciences are an essential step in any systematic inquiry, whether into physical or social or conceptual matters. The humanities—such as literary criticism, number theory, and theology—study categories, such as good/bad, lyric/epic, twelve-tone/melodic, red giant/white dwarf, hominid/*Homo sapiens*, God/gods, prime/not, consciousness/not, exist/not. The crucial and neglected point in the battle of the two cultures is that you have to know what your categories *are* by well-considered definitions, such as *Homo sapiens sapiens*/*Homo sapiens neanderthalensis*, before you can *count* their members. This is obvious—though not to the antihumanistic George Stiglers or Michael C. Jensens or Murray Rothbards among economists.

For example, economic theory is entirely and appropriately humanistic, dealing with definitions and their relations, sometimes called "theorems" or, more usefully for an empirical science, "derivations." Theory says things about categories. Ronald Coase said that transaction costs may be important, and this is how they should be defined. Irving Fisher and Milton Friedman said that MV may equal PT. Francis Y. Edgeworth and Samuelson said that $(dU/dx)/(dU/dy)$ may equal $\$P_x/\$P_y$. The Austrian economists such as Ludwig von Mises, and a miscellany of non-Austrians such as Keynes and Michał Kalecki and George Shackle, said that markets may be more about events out of equilibrium than in equilibrium. Israel Meir Kirzner in theory and now Deirdre Nansen McCloskey in economic history say that discovery may be more important for human progress than is routine accumulation or routine maximization of known functions or routine institutions—they may be necessary gears in the watch but are not the motivating spring.

At the level of economic theorizing, all such scientists are humanists, dealing in categories and derivations, in advance of (though often in lieu of) examining the history of actual markets. Jean Tirole's (Nobel Prize 2014) textbook in 2006 on the theory of finance gathers some hundreds of theories with no evidence supplied about which of the theories might apply to actual financial markets.[2] For good or ill, his book is as much an exercise in humanism as is Kant's *Critique of Pure Reason* or Ramunajan's notebooks on number theory.

Some definitions and their corresponding theorems are wise and helpful, some stupid and misleading. The humanities, and the humanistic step in any science, study such questions, offering more or less sensible arguments for a proposed category being wise or stupid, in advance of the counting or comparison or other factual inquiry into the world. The humanities are the study of the human mind and its curious products, such as John Milton's *Paradise Lost* or Mozart's Concerto for Flute and Harp (K. 299) or the set of all prime pairs or the definition of GDP. The studies depend on categories, such as enjambed/run-on lines or single/double concerti or prime/not-prime numbers or marketed/unmarketed products, such as we humans use. God doesn't tell us. We do.

In the early twentieth century, for example, many economists and other scientists, such as the great British statistician Karl Pearson, believed that the category "Aryan race" was wise and helpful for thinking about the economy and the society. A late example of Pearson's views is in 1925: "Taken on the average, and regarding both sexes, this alien Jewish population is somewhat inferior physically and mentally to the native population." And an early one is his in 1900: "From a bad stock can come only bad offspring."[3] Around then, the American Progressives, and especially among them the leading economists, believed passionately in such racism and advocated policies such as immigration restrictions (later passed into law with the kind assistance of the Ku Klux Klan) and the minimum wage (still defended by modern Progressives) and compelled sterilizations ("Three generations of imbeciles are enough," said Justice Oliver Wendell Holmes Jr. in 1927) to achieve eugenic results perfecting the Aryan race.[4] Later we decided, after some truly disturbing experiences and additional reflection, that "race," aside from *Homo sapiens sapiens*, was actually a stupid and misleading and even evil category. The decision itself depended on reflections on the humanistic categories of helpful/misleading, wise/stupid, good/evil.

The necessity of the humanistic first step, note well, applies to physical and biological sciences as much as to *les sciences humaines* or *die Geisteswissenschaften*. Meaning is scientific because scientists are humans, asking questions interesting to them, such as about the import of β decay. Such is the main conclusion of science studies since Thomas Kuhn. The Danish physicist Niels Bohr wrote in 1927, "It is wrong to think that the task of physics is to find out what the world is. Physics concerns what we can *say* about it."[5] We. Humans. Say. With words. About such *geisteswissenschaftliche* categories the German American poet Rose Ausländer wrote in 1981, "In the beginning / was the word /and the word was with God. / And God gave us the word / and we lived in the word. / And the word is our dream / and the dream is our life."[6]

We dream of categories in our metaphors and our stories, or in our theories and our facts, constrained by what is out in the world and what is inside our dreams. With them we make our models and our economic histories and our lives, especially our scientific lives, saying the world. The poet Wallace Stevens exclaims to his companion, walking on a beach in Key West, "Oh! Blessed rage for order, pale Ramon, / The maker's rage to order words of the sea," the human arrangement of words imposing order on the world's blooming, buzzing confusion. Of the woman they had heard singing along the beach, Stevens sings, "when she sang, the sea, / Whatever self it had, became the self / That was her song, for she was the maker."[7] (Stevens, classically educated, was here noting that Greek *poiemis*, whence our word *poem*, means "maker," for example of a lyric sung.)

There is nothing scary or crazy or French or postmodern or nihilistic about such thoughts. The "hardest" sciences rely on human categories and therefore on human rhetoric and hermeneutics, the speaking and the listening sides of human conversation in the sciences. The category of "capital accumulation," for example, can be defined in an aggregate, Smithian-Marxist-Keynesian way. Or it can be defined in a disaggregated, action-specific Austrian way. The defining matters to the science, changing what we then proceed to measure, or at any rate proceed to talk about and to recommend by way of policy or lack of policy. The Keynesian definition fits well with a policy of the socialization of investment put in the hands of wise governmental economists.[8] Thus, Keynes in 1936, without evidence, wrote that "the State [note his capitalization], which is in a position to calculate the marginal efficiency of capital-goods on long views and on the basis of the general social advantage, . . . [should take] an ever greater responsibility for directly organizing investment."[9] The Austrian definition fits better with a policy of leaving investors alone because they are best equipped with information about their own projects and are punished if they fail. The humanistic job of economic theory is to ponder such categories, to expose their internal logic, to criticize and refine them, just as happens daily in the departments of English and of physics.   .

But the humanistic step—though I am saying it is quite necessary for scientific thought—is of course not in a descriptive science like economics the whole scientific job. The point is regularly missed by economists in their fascination with the blessed rage for order. Theory is not science tout court. One could have a theory of epics or concerti that never applied to any actual epic or concerto and indeed foolishly misrepresented them as they happen to be in the actual human world.

Specializing in humanistic theorizing of the sort that Kenneth Arrow (1921–2017) or Frank Hahn (1925–2013) did is dandy. But it does not do the entire scientifically descriptive job unless it is at some point firmly attached to experiment or observation or introspection or other serious tests against the world—in a way that most of the work of these two brilliant men, Arrow and Hahn on abstract general equilibrium, never was. Arthur Diamond, Jr. looked into its empirical uses. He found none.[10]

This was to be expected. If you are making a quantitative point—as must happen in a world-speaking science like physics or in the glorious, world-speaking systematic inquiry into the past of the business of ordinary life called economic history—then after the humanistic step you must proceed to the actual count of β decay or a testing comparison of Europe with China. Count the European deaths from plague in the late 1340s but then compare its impact in China, from whence it came and where it did similar damage, undermining the mandate of heaven of the Mongol rulers there. Then note, therefore, that a theory of the Great Enrichment after 1750 depending on the shock to the specifically *European* population in 1348 seems doubtful. If it is a good theory, why not the same result in China?

Too often in economics the count or comparison does not happen because economists think, as I have said, that theorems offer factual "insight," and they believe that statistical significance "tests" the theory against the facts. Theory and econometrics, they say, can therefore specialize and specialize and specialize. Never mind actual trade. The procedure is said to imitate physics. But the economists do not inquire into how physics actually works. Physicists, even theorists, as one can see in the lives and writings of Enrico Fermi and Richard Feynman, spend much of their time studying the physical equivalent of the *Journal of Economic History*.

* * *

So what? Here's what. Economic history, and then economics, should become as humanistic as it is now childishly antihumanistic. It will become so when we overcome our anxiety that we might not be worthy of the white coats of the scientists, *Oxford English Dictionary* sense 5b.

Historical economists are well placed to take advantage of humanomics, as for example in merging business and economic history, as William Lazonick has long urged us to do.[11] But to do so, clearly we need to set aside our anxieties about the National Academy of Sciences and listen to *all* the evidence about the economy, whether it comes in the form of statistics of cotton cloth exports or the telegrams of Andrew Carnegie to Henry Frick during the Homestead Strike or the themes of eighteenth-century English drama. That last, for example, is one powerful piece of evidence that in England during the early decades of the eighteenth century, and to a much smaller degree in Germany, Italy, and Spain, the society's attitudes toward business were radically changing.[12]

Our colleagues in economics are trudging off in the other direction with a behaviorist economics that ignores human meaning in favor of insisting in the manner of 1930s psychology that all that matters are external behaviors. Neuroeconomists study the brain but ignore the mind, as though we could understand Jascha Heifetz's violin playing by a closer and closer study of his arm muscles. Similarly, neoinstitutionalism tells the history of a meaningless, mindless Max U—proudly certain that his very meaninglessness is the mark of true science.

The solution for economic historians is not to run after the latest "current policy issue" in the labor market, such as the alleged increase of inequality—though admittedly the temptation to do so is great among young scholars cowed by their present-minded colleagues. The television and newspaper and present politics are poor guides to what is permanently important in the study of the nature and causes of the wealth of nations. If we look at economics or economic history through too narrow a window, we will do the science incorrectly and will damage our fellow citizens. The Chinese communist grandee Chou En-Lai was asked what he thought of the French Revolution. He is supposed to have replied, "It's too early to tell." That's a scientific attitude (though it turns out that he probably thought he was being asked about the very recent upheavals in France in 1968—not so scientific after all). Fogel once told me that his principle in choosing topics for research was to do nothing that would not matter in fifty years. It is why he abandoned early in the 1970s some tentative research into the history of Federal land policy in the United States. More real science.

What will matter in fifty years in economic history is poverty and its ending, and in political history what will matter is tyranny and its ending. If poverty and tyranny are ended, the rest follows. Better stick to the important issues, yes?

CHAPTER FIVE

It's Merely a Matter of Common Sense and Intellectual Free Trade

To put it bluntly, economic history and economics need to wake up. I agree, for example, with an elegant and well-grounded essay by the economic historian Robert Whaples calling for the waking up.[1] Woken-up Robert doesn't say things until he has the goods—and, as he says, we people from the economic side tend to think of the goods as numbers exclusively. It's very true, as he also says, that our numerical habits have repelled the historians in departments of history, especially since they have drifted further into nonquantitative studies of race, class, and gender. Both sides are now far apart and don't read each other with attention. Robert quotes a young historical economist getting the holy trinity slightly wrong, substituting "ethnicity," a very old historical interest, for "class," a reasonably new one. And from the other side, the history historians believe they can adequately study race, class, and gender without using numbers intelligently, beyond page numbers. See, for example, the books by the recent King Cotton School of the history of US slavery, such as that of Sven Beckert, and the devastating quantitative criticism of the work by Alan Olmstead and Paul Rhode.[2] Count on it, the history historian will not listen to counting.

Yet the fierce and ignorant quotations that Robert compiles from economists and economic historians show that quantitative social scientists don't get the point of the humanities. "Whenever I read historians," said a young economic historian to Robert, "my response is: How can you say that without a number? Do you *have* a number?" Many social scientists, and especially those trained as economists, believe adamantly that, as Lord Kelvin put it in 1883, "when you cannot express it in numbers,

your knowledge is of a meager and unsatisfactory kind; it may be the beginning of knowledge, but you have scarcely in your thoughts advanced to
the state of *Science*."[3] The great Frank Knight, the University of Iowa and
University of Chicago economist, said of a version of the motto inscribed
on the social science building at Chicago, "Yes, and when you can't measure, measure anyhow!" Young economists nowadays believe Kelvin's rule
(and Knight's spoof) so fervently, as I did once, that rather than deviating
from their faith they insist on collecting quite meaningless numbers, such
as "statistical significance," or "happiness" on a 1 to 3 scale, or what they
are pleased to call "calibrations" of a hypothetical model unbelievable on
its face. Another Chicago economist, Jacob Viner, said of the Kelvin in-
scription in effect, "Yes, and when you *can* measure your knowledge is of
a meager and unsatisfactory kind!"[4] That's the humility of a true scientist,
one willing to look at all the concepts and evidence.

Kelvin was as arrogant about his physics as many a modern economist
is about his *t*-tests and first-order conditions. On the eve of the discovery
of atomic energy he calculated that Darwin must be wrong because the
sun could not be old enough to have burned long enough from merely
chemical reactions to allow Darwin the hundreds of millions of years he
needed for evolution (Kelvin was sure the sun was no more than twenty
million years old, off by merely a factor of 230). The economists who
laugh at the idea that something might be learned from literature or philosophy are of the same faith, that we are already in specialized posses-
sion of the Truth and need not engage in intellectual trade with anyone
differently endowed. Said one of Robert's faithful, "Why read historians?
They do everything backward. They discuss 'supply' and 'demand' without prices, and speak of needs rather than choices." A just God will pun-
ish such sinners for their foolish pride—a pride that I myself exhibited
at about age twenty-five. In the economic history workshop provided on
Linden Street in Harvard Square by Alexander Gerschenkron for his
graduate students, we pasted over the door a motto, "Give us the data
and we will finish the job." *Oy vey ist mir*. Bless me, father, for I have
sinned.

Agreeing with Robert, I can only make here a point, beyond his as-
signment. It is that if humanistically inclined historians and numbers-and-
math inclined economists are going to work together on their projects of
discovering how society happens—as economics and history themselves
suggest they could profitably do—there needs to come into existence a
humanistic science of economics. Humanomics.

The materialist and antihumanist version of economics, from Marx's surplus value to Douglass North's institutional incentives, cannot explain what one of Robert's interviewees properly called "the miracle of modern economic development." An ethical and rhetorical and ideological and interpersonal change—just what the unscientific humanists study—made the modern world. If true, the finding would be scientifically important. The Victorian travel writer and agnostic Alexander Kinglake suggested that every church should bear on its front door a large sign, "Important If True." So here. Economic history faces no more important question, whether asked by economists or by historians, than why the Great Enrichment and the reduction of mass poverty first started, and especially why it continued. The continuation made us a great deal richer and freer and more capable of human flourishing than our ancestors. The continuations outside of northwestern Europe—continuing now most spectacularly in China and India, of all surprising places—shows that the whole world can be so. It shows, in case you doubted it, that Europe was not special in "race." It shows that, in a world of commercially tested betterment by liberated people, the curse of Malthus lacks force.

The relevance for the silly war on which Robert reports between economists and historians is this: if ideas and ethics and rhetoric (that is, democratic persuasion among a partly free people) contributed largely to such a happy result as the Great Enrichment, then perhaps we should also point our social telescopes toward ideas and ethics and rhetoric. Looking fixedly at trade or imperialism or demography or unions or property law—very interesting though all of them are—will not do the whole of the scientific job. Ideas are the dark matter of history, ignored for a century or so from 1890 to 1980. In those days we were all historical materialists. Even the historians were historical materialists (thus in 1913, for example, Beard's *An Economic Interpretation of the American Constitution*), and the economists have never gotten over it. When anyone suggests that ideas such as the Enlightenment might have had a real effect, as Joel Mokyr has eloquently argued, the economists get *angry*. You can tell when you are stepping on someone's ill-considered dogma, such as in "statistical" significance or in all-encompassing materialism, by his angry and indignant, though feebly argued, response.[5]

To be able to detect and explain the dark matter of ideas we will need a new, idea-acknowledging economics, which would admit, for example, that language shapes an economy. For such a humanistic science of economics, I am arguing, the methods of the human sciences would become as scientifically relevant as the methods of mathematical and statistical sciences now properly are. It would carry out the promise of an economic science such as practiced on occasion by Coase, Gerschenkron, Hayek, Albert Hirschman, Stanley Lebergott, and a relative handful of recent others such as Arjo Klamer and Peter Boettke and Bart Wilson, who use all the evidence. Such a free-trade economic science would scrutinize literary texts *and* simulate on computers, analyze stories *and* model maxima, clarify with philosophy *and* measure with statistics, inquire into the meaning of the sacred *and* lay out the accounting of the profane. The practitioners of the humanities and the social sciences would stop sneering at each other and would start reading each other's books and auditing each other's courses. As their colleagues in the physical and biological sciences so naturally do, they would get down to cooperating for the scientific task.

The economic historian, though, will think, "Oh, dear! I am going to have to learn something new." President Truman said that the worst of experts is someone who doesn't want to learn anything new, because then he wouldn't already be an expert. But to be a good scientist you have to become a scholar and can't remain a specialist in instrumental variables and Max U such as you were on the day you passed your PhD exams. A specialist is not a good scientist. In Ibsen's play of 1891, Hedda Gabler is unhappily married to Professor Tesman, one of two economic historians featured in world literature.[6] She declares to her friend, "Tesman is—a specialist. . . . You should just try it! To hear of nothing but the history of civilization, morning, noon, and night. . . . And then all this about the domestic industry of the Middle Ages!"[7]

It's not so very difficult to get beyond being a specialist in the domestic industry of the Middle Ages, as one can see in the education of graduate students. A bright humanist can learn enough mathematics and statistics in a couple of years to follow their uses in economics. A bright economist, with rather more difficulty, can in a couple of years learn enough about rhetoric and close reading to follow their uses in English. What prevents such scientific cooperation is sneering ignorance, not the difficulty of the task.

When it happens, we will have a fully scientific economics, which will be able to learn from history, and economists will again hire people who are not vague about when the American Civil War began or when England achieved good property rights, or use the phrase "That's pretty philosophical" as a term of contempt or "Theory says that X" as a term of commendation.

So long as economics embodies naively antihumanistic convictions, though, the historians and the economists are going to be mutually repelled, like the magnets that Kelvin studied, or like the nontrading nations that Peter Navarro imagines. Let us pray for the rise of common sense and a respectful trade in ideas as against prideful ignorance and intellectual autarchy.

CHAPTER SIX

After All, Sweet Talk Rules a Free Economy

L et me give the empirical data on the concrete example I've already mentioned—the aggregate, quantitative evidence for taking seriously the role of sweet talk in the economy and therefore taking seriously the role of the humanities. The humanities are rigorous talk about sweet talk.

The evidence is, I asserted, that roughly a quarter of wage income in a society of free people is earned from merely bourgeois and feminine persuasion—not orders or information, but persuasion, the changing of minds. It is not merely a change in behavior achieved in other ways, as by physical coercion ("Your money or your life") or even by monetary incentives ("You're fired"). Among a free people it is largely instead sweet talk.

One thinks immediately of advertising, but advertising is a tiny part of the total. Advertising, or commercial free speech, irritates the clerisy because the clerisy doesn't like the tasteless stuff purchased by *hoi polloi*, not one bit. Better: an adventure holiday watching birds in Antarctica or a tasteful pied-à-terre in the West Village or buying lovely books on bettering humanomics. The American clerisy has been saying since Veblen that the many are in the grips of a tiny group of advertisers who fool them into buying tasteless schlock. So the purchases of Coke and gas grills and automobiles are the result of hidden persuasion or, to use a favorite word of the clerisy, an amazingly efficacious *manipulation*.

To a Marshallian/Austrian economist the peculiarly American attribution of gigantic powers to thirty-second television spots is puzzling. If advertising had the powers attributed to it by the clerisy, then unlimited fortunes could be had from the mere writing. "It's toasted." Yet advertising is less than 2 percent of gross domestic product, and much of it is uncontroversially informative and unmanipulative, such as shop signs, entries on web pages, and ads in trade magazines aimed at highly sophisticated buyers.[1] When Vance Packard in 1957 published his attack on advertising, *The Hidden Persuaders*, he thought he would lose his friends on Madison Avenue. But they were delighted. An account executive friend would come up and say, "Vance, before your book I had a hard time persuading my clients that advertising worked. Now they think it's magic."

How then to determine how big is sweet talk in a society of free contracting? Take a list of detailed categories of employment and make a guess as to the percentage of the time in each spent on persuasion. For example, read down the roughly 250 occupations listed in "Employed Civilians by Occupation" (table 602) in the *Statistical Abstract of the United States 2007* looking for the jobs that involve a good deal of sweet-talking, or on the contrary the jobs without any.[2] The 125,000 "appraisers and assessors of real estate" are not, in an honest economy, open to human persuasion, as any American knows who has had a house appraised. The 243,000 firefighters also just do their jobs, with little talk—although one sees here the depth of sweet talk in a modern economy, or for that matter a nonmodern economy, because a firefighter in a burning building does actually a good deal of talking and sometimes engages in urgent persuasion. The 121,000 aircraft pilots and flight engineers persuade us to keep our seat belts fastened until the plane arrives at the gate and the seat-belt sign is turned off. That's a very small part of their job, but consider the big supervisory roles they often assume as captains, and the sweet talk needed to keep the crew cooperating. And consider the disasters attributable to cultural differences in talking persuasively to the control tower. The straight talk common to the West is often seen as impolite in the East, and there are documented cases of crashes caused by squeamishness about appearing to be too abrupt in speech when asking permission for an emergency landing. But set such occupations aside as nonpersuasive.

The 1,491,000 construction laborers are not known for persuasive language, except in the old days when a pretty girl walked by, such as Dil in the movie *The Crying Game*. But anyone who has actually worked in such a job knows the necessity of getting cooperation from your mates, persuading the boss that all is well, being a regular guy or gal. It's sweet talk, or else the job site breaks down. But again set such jobs aside.

Out of the 142 million civilians employed in 2005 (these figures don't change much in their proportions over time, and it's proportions we seek), it seems reasonable to assign 100 percent of the hours of the 1,031,000 lawyers and judges to persuading, preparing to persuade, or being an audience for persuasion. And likewise that of the 154,000 public relations specialists and the large number of "social, recreational, and religious workers," such as counselors, social workers, and clergy—a total of 2,138,000 of them persuading people how to live. All right, if you doubt it, set it as low as 90 percent—but high.

Managers and supervisors of various sorts are the biggest category to which it seems reasonable to assign a lower but still high figure, say, 75 percent of labor income earned from sweet talk. In a free society the workers cannot be peremptorily ordered about and beaten with knouts if they do not respond. They need to be persuaded. What the US Census Bureau styles "managerial occupations," such as George Halvorson, once chairman and CEO of Kaiser Permanente, or Daniel R. McCloskey, once a senior national account executive for Illy Coffee North America, are a massive 14.7 million, fully 10 percent of the labor force. David Lodge's novel *Nice Work* shows a lecturer in English, Robyn Penrose, realizing that the managing director she was assigned to "shadow" was first and last a persuader: "It did strike [her] sometimes that Vic Wilcox stood to his subordinates in the relation of teacher to pupils. . . . She could see that he was trying to *teach* the other men, to coax and persuade them to look at the factory's operations in a new way. . . . It was so deftly done that she had sometimes to temper her admiration by reminding herself that it was all directed by the profit-motive."[3] (The sneer at the profit motive is that of the character, not the author; it is conveyed here by what literary people call Jane Austen–type "free indirect style.")

The "first-line supervisors" scattered over all sectors (construction, personal services, gambling)—whom I suppose similarly to be earning 75 percent of their income from persuasion—would add another 5.5 million. I worked at highway construction during summers in college and know how sweet-and-sour talking (but anyway talking) that Glenn, the skilled foreman from Missouri, had to exercise to get the asphalt raked right. Add another 380,000 for personal financial advisors, plus the 150,000 editors and (merely) 89,000 news analysts, reporters, and correspondents— bearing in mind the explosion since 2005, and thus not included in these figures, of bloggers and other self-employed *journalistas* vying for attention with their own sweet talk, sometimes paid. Journalists mostly imagine themselves to be doing "straight reporting," that noble dream of objectivity. But it doesn't take much rhetorical education to realize that they must select their facts persuasively and report them interestingly in sweet words. Likewise, the enormous category of salespeople (13.4 million, which excludes the 3.1 million cashiers), though also on duty to prevent shoplifting, can reasonably be accounted as 75-percent sweet talkers. "The dress is *you*, dear." It may even be true. In my experience, actually, it usually is. With our strange suspicion since the seventeenth century in Europe about rhetoric, we exaggerate the amount of lying that salespeople engage in, at any rate in a society that honors ethical behavior in such matters (as bargaining economies do not).

Among 50-percent persuaders we can count loan councilors and officers (429,000: as with judges in courts of law, they are professional audiences for persuasion, saying yes or no after listening to your sweet talk and gathering your information); human resources, training, and labor relations (660,000: "Mr. Babbitt, I just don't think you have much of a future at Acme"; consider George Clooney as the hire-to-fire consultant in *Up in the Air*); writers and authors (we are merely 178,000, but think again of the tens of thousands of people who work at it in blogs and writers' groups without publication, though also without payment figuring in national accounts, though a correct set of national accounts would include their costly satisfactions too); claims adjusters and investigators (303,000); and, a very big category, the 8,114,000 educational, training, and library occupations, such as college professors (we are 1.2 million alone) and nursery school teachers. "Don't plagiarize your term paper, Ms. Jones." "Play nice, Johnny."

Perhaps a mere quarter of the effort of the 1,313,000 police and sheriff's patrol officers, detectives, criminal investigators, correctional officers, and private detectives is spent on persuasion, though the ones I've talked to put the figure higher. Look at Ferguson, Missouri, in 2014 for the difference from one evening to the next in the persuasiveness of the police. Night and day.

In health care, as anyone who has worked in it knows, sweet talk is important—advocating for the patient, getting him to stay on his blood-pressure medicine, talking sweetly with other caregivers, dealing with insurance companies and hospital administrators (some of whom are included above in the managerial category). In the large category "health care practitioners and technical occupations," we can remove from the realm of persuasion the technical occupations—X-ray technicians, medical records technicians, and so forth—although even these can't merely silently work, if they work well. The technician at the eye doctor keeps saying to you, "Good, that's right. Turn your head up a little. Good. Watch the blue dot. Good. Hold it." Sweet talk. For the physicians, dentists, nurses, speech therapists, and so forth who actually talk to patients and to each other—a total of 7,600,000 health-care talkers—it seems reasonable to say that persuading accounts for a quarter of their economic value. Perform a mental experiment. Try to imagine a speech therapist—an occupation I know well—with no persuasive skills whatever, a mere transmitter of the information that, say, a child need not be ashamed of being a stutterer when stuttering includes Winston Churchill and Margaret Drabble and Marilyn Monroe and Joe Biden. Imagine how much less valuable she or he would be without sweet talk. The 353,000 paralegals and legal assistants count in the one-quarter category too. A quarter sounds low.

The occupations mentioned, without hunting in supposedly nonpersuasive categories such as mail carriers or bus drivers or "life, physical, and social science occupations" (within which are classed many of the persuasive economists and law professors themselves), amount to 36,100,000 equivalent workers (that is, the number of 90-percent persuaders multiplied by 0.9, 75-percenters by 0.75, 50-percenters by 0.5, and one-quarter persuaders by 0.25, all added up). For 2007 (to which I am applying the 2005 categories), that's an astonishing quarter of the income-earning private employees in the United States. It would be higher if weighted instead by dollar incomes, considering the large number of managers and supervisors (about 20 million, remember, out of the 142 million workers). Managers are of course higher paid compared to the people they persuade to work hard.

In short, a quarter of our labor incomes attributed to sweet talk is a lower bound. Similar calculations for 1988 and 1992, using the slightly different categories available for those years, yielded similar results.[4] Somewhat surprisingly the weight of sweet talk in the economy does not seem to have much risen since then—though if police and health-care workers were put in the 50-percent category and educators in the 75 percent category, as the 1988/1992 calculations assumed, the share of persuasive work in 2005 would nudge up to 28.4 percent of the total. The Australian economist Gerry Antioch has redone the figures for the United States and arrives for 2009 at 30 percent.[5]

*   *   *

The calculation could be improved with more factual and economic detail. Among a hundred other fruitful scientific projects in humanomics one can imagine, it would make a very good PhD thesis. For instance, as

I just said, the workers could be weighted by salaries. The occupational categories could be subdivided. The marginal product of persuasion could be considered in more detail, looking closely at payment for persuasive as against nonpersuasive work. The premium for better persuasion could be estimated from sales commissions or promotions. One way of backing the estimates from the detailed occupational categories would be to do in-depth interviews, probing in each job for sweet talk, as against mere coercion or physical activity or information transmittal. Ride along in squad cars and listen and watch. The managers likewise could be shadowed. It's what Ronald Coase in economics did during the 1930s to discover transaction costs and what Robyn Penrose in fiction did during the 1980s to discover managerial teaching.

Coercion, as against persuasion, would seem in most rich places to be less prevalent now, at least in some ways, than it was in the same places in the eighteenth century. True, coercion in taxation is much higher. Try persuading the IRS to make you a special exception. Slaves or some servants in husbandry were once coerced physically. Yet in olden days a self-employed yeoman farmer or even a farmhand, categories that together would describe in, say, 1800, most free people, was not much coerced or even much supervised. Silas in Frost's poem "Death of the Hired Man" (composed ca. 1905) makes his hay load skillfully the way he wants, and "He's come to help you ditch the meadow. / He has a plan. You mustn't laugh at him." So it's not altogether clear how the long-run balance of compulsion and autonomy has changed. Yet even within the big bureaucracies of the modern state, in free and even in less free countries, and even though financed sometimes by the compulsion of taxes as against voluntary payments to business bureaucracies, sweet talk figures largely, and orders and compulsion are correspondingly less than one might think from, say, Chaplin in *Modern Times*.

On balance the sweet-talking share of national income was probably smaller before the Great Enrichment. More often a manager in 1800 did not have to be a David Lodge teacher. He or she could simply be a tyrant. The commanding lieutenant (not yet captain) William Bligh of the *Bounty* is supposed to have been a case in point ("that *Bounty* bastard," as the sailors later called him in extenuation of their mutiny). (His actual fault appears to have been a discipline-wrecking indulgence toward his crew's desire to tarry in Tahiti.) The captain even of a merchantman, and still more of His Majesty's warship, expected instant obedience, essential when rounding the Horn in a force 9 gale or expecting every man to do his duty at Cape Trafalgar. It's still true in the military, of course, or in military-style businesses in the crisis. The monastic Rule of Benedict required immediate, pride-disciplining obedience. An arrogant pride in oneself instead of worshipping the Lord thy God was the chief sin against the Holy Spirit. Occupations that depended on sweet talk were fewer in olden days. In future days they will be more numerous, as the physical making of things goes to automation of AI, at lower and lower opportunity cost. In the heavenly city of the future the only task left will be deciding what to do, sweetly arguing about it with fellow angels over a beer, or harp.

The result can be checked against other measures. Douglass North and John Wallis reckoned that 50 percent of American national income was Coasean transaction costs, the costs of persuasion being part of these. Expenditures to negotiate and enforce contracts—the Wallis-North definition of transaction costs—rose from a quarter of national income in 1870 to over half in 1970.[6] Their measure is not exactly the one wanted here. Their transaction costs include, for example, "protective services," such as police and prison guards, some of whose income (I am claiming three-quarters of it remaining after sweet talk) is "talk" only in an inappropriately extended, and sometimes physically coercive, sense. Literal talk is special. In particular it is cheap, as guns and locks and walls are not, in a way that makes it analytically separate from the rest of transaction costs. We say, "A word to the wise is sufficient." Sweet talk is the carefully chosen but to a large degree opportunity-cost-free words of persuasion.

The same point can be made from the other side of the national accounts, the product side. The more obviously talky parts of production amount to a good share of the total, and much of it is persuasion rather than information or command. Out of an American domestic product of $11,734 billion in 2004, one can sort through the categories of value added at the level of fifty or so industries, assigning rough guesses as to the percentage of sweet talk produced by each—80 percent for "management of companies," say, or 20 percent for "real estate rental and leasing," or 40 percent for "art and entertainment"—and get up to about 17 percent of total national product, fully consistent with 25 percent of merely labor income. Persuasion is big.[7]

Not all the half of American workers who are white collar do sweet talk for a living, but many do, and more do more of it as office work gets less physical. In the age of word processing, the work of offices has shifted far from physical typing and filing and copying done by women, not to speak of the earlier transition in offices away from Bartleby the Scrivener or Bob Cratchit on a high stool. So, for that matter, have many blue-collar jobs come to involve sweet talk, such as warehousemen persuading each other to handle the cargo just so, as have pink-collar jobs, too, such as waitresses dealing all day with talking people. Debra Ginsberg in her memoir of 2000, *Waiting: The True Confessions of a Waitress*, describes the first minute of contact with the customers as a little stage show determining the tip.

It's not "mere" talk. A good percentage of such talkers are persuaders. The secretary shepherding a document through the company bureaucracy is often called on to exercise sweet talk, and veiled threats. If she can't use talk, sweet or not so sweet, to bend the official institutions of her bureaucracy, she's not doing her job. The bureaucrats and professionals who constitute most of the white-collar workforce are not themselves merchants, but they do a merchant's business of persuasion inside and outside their companies.

A thorough survey of seven thousand workers in the United States by Daniel Pink in 2012 confirmed the result, as reported in his *To Sell Is Human: The Surprising Truth about Moving Others*. "Across a range of professions," he wrote, "we are devoting roughly 24 minutes of every hour to moving others" in nonsales sweet talk, that is, without a purchase.[8] He asked, "What percentage of your work involves convincing or persuading people to give up something they value for something you have?" and got the reply of 41 percent. "The capacity to sell isn't some unnatural adaption to the merciless world of commerce. Selling is fundamentally human."[9] Humans have always made decisions on where to go next to hunt and gather, or to which port to take the olive-oil-filled amphorae, as Matthew Arnold imagined an ancient Greek merchant who landed on the coast of Portugal "and unbent sails / There, where down cloudy cliffs, through sheets of foam, / Shy traffickers, the dark Iberians come; / And on the beach undid his corded bales."

The decisions are not always those of the tyrants in a centralized bureaucracy, such as a sea captain or a university provost or a military general, who won't take counsel. In free societies, whether during our long past as hunter-gatherers before agriculture or during our manufacturing-and-services present, sweet talk rules.

CHAPTER SEVEN

Therefore We Should Walk on Both Feet, Like Ludwig Lachmann

Humanomics suggests, then, that economists might better walk on both feet. Yes, let's also keep walking with the behaviorist, positivist, nonverbal, quantitative foot thrust forward so dogmatically since the 1930s by Robbins, Samuelson, Friedman, Lipsey, Jensen, Becker, and Stigler. But then let's walk also on the other humanistic, cognitive, rhetorical, ethical, hermeneutic, qualitative foot recommended since the 1770s for getting somewhere meaningful at speed by Smith, Mill, Wicksteed, Mises, Schumpeter, Keynes, Knight, Hayek, Boulding, Shackle, Hirschman, Heilbroner, Buchanan, Kirzner, Vaughn, Lavoie, Boettke, Daniel Klein, Virgil Storr, Klamer, B. Wilson, V. Smith, Amariglio, and Ludwig Lachmann.[1]

You might notice the prominence of Austrian economists and their fellow travelers in the humanistic list. Let me make explicit the point I've been hinting at, trying to persuade the Austrians and the neoinstitutionalists (not entirely overlapping groups) to turn seriously to the humanities, as the Austrians in a tentative way already do.

Yes, I know. If you are an orthodox, Samuelsonian economist not acquainted with Austrian economics, you are liable to yawn and turn away. I had the same attitude for decades after graduate school. Austrian economics is not mathematical enough, you will think, to yield a publication in the *American Economic Review*. That is as it may be. But if you want to do serious economic science, as against careerism without principle, you would do well to crack the books by Boettke or Kirzner or Hayek or Mises. Subscribe to Don Boudreaux's *Café Hayek* blog. Listen, really listen, Peace to the *AER* (on the editorial board of which I served a bit when Joe Stiglitz ran the show; I couldn't stand the dreary pile of existence theorizing and meaningless tests of significance, and withdrew). But you are a serious student of the economy, and seek truth—wherever it leads, yes?

A case in point is Ludwig Lachmann (1906–1990), the last student of the German Historical School economist Werner Sombart and one of the first students of the Austrian economist Ludwig von Mises. He is not a perfect instrument for arguing for the humanities in economics and for a full humanomics. He could issue such conventional ukases as "The real nature of truth, the ultimate grounds of human existence, the universal criteria of the Good and the Beautiful, are the province of the philosopher, not of the scientist. For this very reason the economist, as an economist, must refrain from making value-judgements."[2] Pretty weak tea, and it's strange for a native German speaker to adopt the modern English definition of science as against *Wissenschaft*. But on other grounds Lachmann is a better humanist even than some of the older Austrians. Most of them, including Lachmann, were educated in the classical *gymnasia* of *Mitteleuropa*. The humanism of such an education seemed to have influenced Lachmann more deeply.

I have claimed that the techniques of the humanities have serious scientific status in the using and criticizing of economic stories and metaphors, such as the prisoner's dilemma or the tragedy of the commons or the business school conviction that incentives are trumps.[3] After all, it is humans we are construing, not rats or computer programs, which is something that Lachmann vividly understood. Lachmann, like many economic Austrians—and unlike neoinstitutionalists and for that matter most other economists since the 1930s—boldly faced humans and human meaning, what he called "internal" matters as against externals such as institutions. He did not hop painfully along on his behaviorist foot by itself, toppling over from time to time.[4] True, like many Austrian economists, Lachmann may have undervalued what can be achieved even by mere behaviorism. But at least he knew he had two feet.

Yet surely, the orthodox Samuelsonian will reply, *De gustibus non est disputandum*, of tastes one should not dispute. Surely the economist, as an economist, must refrain from making value judgments, the province of the philosopher. Surely the scientific method one heard about in high school chemistry requires one to eschew discussion of ends and to focus merely on means, yes?

No. I have raised the issue before. It is *not* true, in Lachmann's unhappy formulation, that the economist, as an economist, must refrain from making value judgments. On the contrary, *De gustibus* finibusque *est disputandum*, of tastes *and ends* we *should* dispute, if we want a social science worthy of the name, walking on two feet. In an interview Lachmann said, "My impression from reading certain recent Chicago publications such as the famous article, '*De Gustibus Non Est Disputandum*' (*AER*, March, 1977), is that these economists don't understand the difference between action and reaction. They seem unwilling to admit that there is such a thing as spontaneous action in the world."[5] Action is about ends and value judgments. Positivism is about reaction, not the free will of human action. React to a budget line, the rules of the game. No hope or love or courage. No free will.

Positivism, to be sure, is fine as one among many rhetorical devices in making a scientific case in economics. It is only when it becomes a foundational and exclusive dogma that it goes wrong. It's that way with any virtue. Without temperance and love, justice is cruel. Without courage, hope is a dead letter.[6] One therefore can conjure with national income statistics and yet also believe that spontaneous human actions matters deeply in entrepreneurship, in finance, in the pioneering of consumption (rich men's playthings like bicycles and autos, and recently even ocean pleasure cruises, became the tools and consumption of the *demos*), in commercially tested betterment generally. There is no reason to choose, and certainly no philosophical reason. Through humanomics the news of the death of positivism is finally now arriving in our economic precincts (I tried in the 1980s and 1990s to bring the good news from Ghent to Aix but failed).

In academic psychology, behaviorism reached its vigorous maturity, I have noted, during the 1930s, recording reactions of dogs to bells and of rats to food pellets. But then it promptly died of a cognitive heart attack, a little before economists started to perform behaviorist experiments on rats and pigeons.[7] The economic experimenters did not realize that showing animals to be rational from watching their observable responses to budget lines merely showed how strange and inhuman the definition of the word *rational* had become in economics. One might better take a humanistic hint from what is called in philosophy the Oxford School of "ordinary language" philosophy—of Gilbert Ryle and J. L. Austin using ordinary language as a philosophical mining site—and therefore ask what *rationality* might properly mean. It surely means understanding the difference between action and reaction and admitting that there is such a thing as spontaneous action in the world. It does not mean satisfying the weak axiom of revealed preference, not in ordinary language. It means "humanly reasonable," responding to argument and free will, which only in a much reduced sense would apply to rats and pigeons, or for that matter to computer programs.

The by now ageing behavioral economics—any findings yet shown empirically to wreck markets in nationally significant magnitudes?—which was also inspired by 1930s behaviorism, attempted once again to revive the notion that we can best study humans by focusing on individual behavior as against the Lachmannian market. Behaviorism pretends that we don't know what's going on in human heads, claiming that we ourselves are not inside human minds, assuming that there is nothing to be learned from four thousand years of written reports of human minds and declaring that we can only "predict" behavior from the outside by posing tricky inferential questions showing humans to be incompetent at probability theory. The "naturalist" turn in neuroeconomics, I have noted, is similar. It claims that the mind is the brain, a hypothesis for which there is no evidence. It was given answer in the late seventeenth century by Andrew Marvell in his poem "The Garden":

> The mind, that ocean where each kind
> Does straight its own resemblance find,
> Yet it creates, transcending these,
> Far other worlds, and other seas;
> Annihilating all that's made
> To a green thought in a green shade.

The Austrians like Lachmann understand the import of such lines. (They are not, I have said, the Austrians like Murray Rothbard, who attacked Lachmann and his students such as Don Lavoie as "nihilists" because they used ideas of hermeneutics and rhetoric, that is, strayed from cargo-cult science in a humanistic direction.) Lachmann would have understood, too, a philosopher's remark that consciousness is characterized by "the liberty of its conceptual and imaginative powers from the constraints of its material circumstances." It creates, transcending these—which Lachmann called spontaneous action. The philosopher continued: "Within the mechanistic view . . . causality is no more than mindless force [such as reaction to Max U under constraints] and so the causal power of seemingly immaterial things like . . . volition or final purposes creates a deep problem."[8] You're telling me. The ghost in the machine, the soul in the brain, runs the show.

*   *   *

One of Lachmann's heroes was Max Weber. In Lachmann's little book of 1971, *The Legacy of Max Weber*, he riffs on Weber's antibehaviorist methods. As early as 1907, in an article titled "The Paradigm of the Skat Game" (*skat* is a German card game), Weber had attacked the metaphor of society governed by the Northian phrase "the rules of the game," employed at the time by the legal philosopher Rudolf Stammler. "An institution," Lachmann writes, "provides means of orientation to a large number of actors. It enables them to coordinate their actions by means of orientation to a common signpost."[9] The institution is not a dispositive rule of the game but merely a sign, always to be interpreted, like a traffic light. Thus, too, our clothing is an institution, and so is language, and of course so are price "signals," as we economists say. They are not mechanical in their outcomes.

Lachmann summarizes Weber's attack on Stammler (and, one might say, had he but known, on North) as "Norms as such cannot determine a concrete outcome."[10] The rules of chess do not imply a solution. In tic-tac-toe, by contrast, assuming mild rationality, they do. Noting that Weber was trained as a lawyer, Lachmann quotes him on legal change: "The really decisive element," Weber had written, "has always been a *new line of conduct* which then results either in a change of the meaning of the existing rules of law or in the creation of new rules of law."[11] It is one of the main weaknesses, among many, of neoinstitutionalism that it does not have a closed theory of legal change yet assumes that change *is* closed, with a snap. In many important matters the law is not closed—it is not tic-tac-toe—which is why we have appellate courts. Look at the evolving doctrines from the US Supreme Court on the commerce clause or the first amendment or Title VII of the Civil Rights Act of 1964. We need a way to talk about these that does not reduce them to tic-tac-toe, input and output.

In his book on Weber, Lachmann criticizes his own master, Menger (he is referring to app. 6 in Menger, *Grundsätze der Volkswirtschaftslehre* [1871]), for his economistic "needs theory" of institutions—which is North's functionalism. "The weakness of this theory," Lachmann notes, "lies in its failure to provide us with any criterion by which to distinguish between those needs which will find their satisfaction through appropriate institutions and those which will not."[12]

It is a rare fault in Jared Rubin's recent, brilliant book on why Islam did not yield economic growth that he cannot explain why the need for economic growth did not find satisfaction in appropriate economic institutions.[13] The syllogism of neoinstitutionalism is that institutions are (merely material) incentives. Following (economic) incentives raises income. Therefore, institutions caused modern economic growth. The unanswered question, before even asking whether the institutions have the quantitative oomph to cause very much economic growth, is why the prospect of growth did not change the institutions. Why do institutions sometimes create such incentives but sometimes inspire reaction? And why do humans so often act against incentives, the way John Hancock boldly signed the Declaration of Independence, a hanging offense. It's not closed.

Lachmann continues: "Weber's approach to social action is something very different from that of the structural-functional theories. Weber was concerned with the *meaning* the actor attributes to his action. Most social-system theories ignore this aspect of action."[14] Behaviorism does, for example. Yet even Menger conceived of entities in society as giving life to the social world, all depending on human valuation à la the humanities. Like the philosopher John Searle's suggestive writings on social constructions, good old Menger saw meaning emerging from social agreements.[15] Utterances. Language games. Ethics. All of them are radically unpredictable in outcome, which is Rubin's problem in distinguishing the European alliance of religion and politics in the divine right of kings from the similar but fatally antieconomic Islamic alliance, such as the deal in 1744 between Wahhabi Islam and the House of Saud. If institutions caused economic growth, it would be easy for economists to design them or undesign them. If economists were so smart, to say it again, they would be rich. A certain modesty seems appropriate.

The economist Jacob Viner said in 1950,

A great part of true learning, in fact, takes the form of negative knowledge, of increasing awareness of the range and depth of our unconquered ignorance, and it is one of the major virtues of scholarship that only by means of it, one's own or someone else's, can one know when it is safe to dispense with it. Learned ignorance, therefore, is often praiseworthy, although ignorant learning . . . never is.[16]

That's right.

CHAPTER EIGHT

That Is, Economics Needs Theories of Human Minds beyond Behaviorism

Time therefore to stop and reflect. Time therefore to cease believing that only a reactive scientific and mechanistic materialism governs the human world and to start acknowledging that there is such a thing as human, spontaneous action, what the theologians call free will. Time to let the humanities into economic science without abandoning any of the mathematics or statistics, or at any rate the parts that make economic sense.

What physicists found unusual about Enrico Fermi (1901–1954) is that he did both, the mathematical, qualitative, categorizing, humanistic theorizing on the one hand and the simulating, quantifying, factual, practical experimenting on the other, and he did both at a Nobel Prize level. For example, the question came up in casual conversation among a group of physicists including Fermi whether there were advanced civilizations elsewhere in the universe. As the others kept on chattering, Fermi fell silent for a few minutes, doing in his head what later became known as a Drake calculation. He arrived silently at a very high estimate of the probable number of such civilizations. Then he broke his silence with a challenge: "Well, where *is* everybody?" If such civilizations existed in the numbers implied by rough guesses at how many habitable planets there were, he was reasoning, they long had world enough and time since the big bang for a very large number of them to have developed exceedingly advanced technology, in which case they would *already* be speaking to us. Something is wrong, he implied, with the supposition that we are *not* alone. (Leo Szilard, a Hungarian physicist in the group, gave a witty reply, which did not however diminish the theoretical and empirical profundity Fermi had just exhibited: "Enrico, they are already speaking to us. We just call them 'Hungarians,'" such as Teller, Wigner, and Szilard.[1])

Such is the merit of numbers. If you know, for example, that real income per head has risen in Europe since 1800 by a factor of about thirty, then your political impulse to condemn "capitalism" as impoverishing or riddled with "imperfections" is at least disciplined. You may continue to be a socialist or a regulator, but you will need to sharpen your argument in some other way than going on and on using the same alternative false facts and fake science of impoverishment and imperfection. We need numbers and we need words, both, Fermi style.

*　*　*

Here then is a fuller example of incomplete economic science, an example about which Lachmann had something to say, and which I have a great deal more to say in the other book of this pair, *Beyond Behaviorism*. Some economists grasp that institutions have to do with human meaning, not merely Northian "constraints." The Austrians and the old institutionalists managed to escape, Houdini-like, from the straightjacket that Douglass North, Gary Becker, Deepak Lal, Avner Greif, Steven Levitt, Max U, and their friends have so eagerly donned. Lachmann spoke of "certain super-individual schemes of thought, namely, *institutions*, to which schemes of thought of the first order, the plans, must be oriented, and which serve therefore, to some extent, the coordination of individual plans."[2] Notice that according to the Austrians the economy, being about the future, simply *is* thought, all the way down. Thus, a courtroom of the common law is a scheme of thought backed by propriety and bailiffs and law books. It coordinates individual plans. Thus, too, a language is a scheme of thought backed by ethics and social approval and conversational implicatures. It, too, coordinates individual plans. Such language games are much more observable, to revert to positivist jargon, than the contents of utility functions: just listen to human utterances. Indeed, the subjectivist turn in economic theorizing in the 1870s, Lachmann averred, implied that the economy was a matter of utterances of individual human minds. The utterances were directed at other humans sweet-talking about their plans, not solipsistic remarks such as "I think, therefore I am."

Silent maximizing is a virtue, to be sure. It is the virtue characteristic of a human seeking profit—yet also, I have already noted, of a rat seeking cheese and of a blade of grass seeking light. What is grasped by

Lachmann, and the new American Austrian economists inspired by him during his visits from 1973 to 1987 to New York, is that prudence is surely important, just the ticket for understanding entry and exit, say, but that meaning is imparted to human lives by the *non*prudential virtues and by the speech that enacts or discusses them.

After all, temperance and courage and love and justice and hope and faith are also virtues, and they are the ones *defining* humans. Unlike prudence, which as I have by now repeatedly noted characterizes every form of life and quasi life down to viruses, the nonprudence virtues are characteristic of humans pretty much uniquely and of human languages and their constructed meanings. (I except elephants mourning their dead and chimps indignant at not getting the grape their fellow gets.) A mortal knows of her death and speaks and acts in its light, for which no immortal god would see the need. An immortal would have no need for courage or hope or temperance and little enough for love or justice or faith. The Greek tales of the gods reflect precisely their amoral character. And to speak of other creatures, in no sense is a prudent blade of grass "courageous" or a prudent rat "faithful" (outside of the movie *Ratatouille*, whose humor turns on the irony that the rat hero is more faithful, and less motivated by prudence only, than many of the humans). In 1725 Bishop Samuel Butler complained about "the strange affection of many people of explaining away all particular affections and representing the whole of life as nothing but one continued exercise of [prudent] self-love."[3] Compare recently the late, great Gary Becker.

Or as another of the greats, Hugo de Groot (Grotius) put it in 1625, "The saying that every creature is led by nature to seek its own private advantage, expressed thus universally, must not be granted. . . . [The human animal] has received from nature a peculiar instrument, that is, the use of speech; I say that he has besides that a faculty of knowing and acting [thus again Mises and Lachmann: human action] according to some general principles; so that what relates to this faculty is not common to all animals, but properly and peculiarly agrees to mankind."[4] Contrast again North and his followers, who will have none of particular affections and human speech and meanings and acting according to some general principle aside from one's self-love. The behaviorist formulas of constraints and rules of the game miss what North could have learned from Lachmann, Geertz, Weber, Smith, Aquinas, Cicero, Confucius, Moses, or his mother (North's mother, or Moses's)—that social rules expressed in human languages have human meanings. They are instruments as well as constraints, as Lachmann says, playthings as well as fences, communities as much as mental-ward rules.[5]

Take, for example, so trivial an institution for providing incentives and coordinating individual plans as a traffic light. When it turns red, it surely does create a material incentive to stop. For one thing, the rule is self-enforcing, because the cross traffic has the green. (In the joke, a New York City taxi driver drives at high speed through every red light but screeches to a halt at every green. His terrified passenger demands to know why. "Today my brother is driving, too, and he *always* goes through red lights!") For another, the police may be watching, or the automatic camera may capture your license plate. The red light is a fence, a constraint, a rule of the game, or of the mental ward. So far goes North, and with him most Samuelsonian economists.

Yet the red light has meaning to humans, who are more than rats in a prudence-only experiment facing food incentives. Among other things it means the state's dominance over drivers. It signals the presence of civilization and the ever-contested legitimacy granted to the state that a civilization entails. (Suppose you are struggling through a pathless jungle and come upon . . . a traffic light: "Mr. Civilization, I presume.") It signals, too, the rise of mechanical means of regulation. As Lachmann, who spent most of his career in South Africa, would have known, the Afrikaans language calls the traffic light *'n robot*, in contrast to a human traffic officer with white gloves on a concrete stand.

The red light is in Lachmann's terms a system of thought that works with greater or lesser efficacy to coordinate human action. But it also *means* something to the human, and the meaning can matter greatly to the economic or political parts of their lives. The traffic light is a system that some drivers find comforting and others find irritating, depending on their attitudes toward the state or toward mechanical inventions such as robots or toward traffic officers. For a responsible citizen, or an Iowan, or indeed for a fascist conformist, the green or red light means the keeping of rules. She will wait for the green even at 3:00 a.m. at an intersection obviously clear in all directions, an intersection lacking a license-plate camera or police person in attendance or a reliably irresponsible brother on the road even when she's in a bit of a hurry. Incentives be damned. But for a principled social rebel, or a Bostonian, or indeed for a sociopath, the light is a challenge to his autonomy, a state-sponsored insult. Again, incentives be damned. If the broken-window policy of policing, for example, is applied *too* vigorously, it could well evoke an angry reaction from potential criminals, or even peaceable folk, and could result in more, not less, crime, or at any rate widespread resentment of the police. Sometimes it has.

I learned after I wrote this that the American sociologist Erving Goffman in 1961 made the same point about traffic lights. Of course. Behavior is not just behavior. To the people involved, in the situation they believe they are in, it has meaning. Recall Ausländer: "we lived in the word. / And the word is our dream / and the dream is our life."

*   *   *

How, then, do you stay on the scientific rails once the humanistic job of classification is done?[6] You do it by adding measurement used in a positivistic way. A science of magnitude like economics needs the humanistic theorizing and then the quantitative measuring. The one gives meaning and content to the other. "Thoughts without content [*Inhalt*] are empty [*leer*], intuitions without concepts are blind [*blind*]," said Kant. He continued: "It is, therefore, just as necessary to make the mind's concepts sensible—that is, to add an object to them in intuition—as to make our intuitions understandable—that is, to bring them under concepts. . . . The understanding can intuit nothing, the senses can think nothing. Only from their unification can cognition arise."[7]

You are not to lose sight of humanistic understanding, Weber's *verstehen*, the view out from the human soul as against the view from outside of the behavior of the human body. Lachmann and other Austrian economists have, for example, a lively appreciation of the humanity of businesspeople. Capital is not measurable as an aggregate, Lachmann writes, because "different segments of the minds of different manager-entrepreneurs [find] expression in the specific compositions of their capital combinations."[8] It's minds all the way down. As he says in another essay, "Each owner's judgment of his investment expenditure . . . rests on a subjective expectation about the future."[9] It is an idea, an "act of mind," as he puts it. The investments are arrayed in human minds from best to least profitable, the last investment actually undertaken in view of its opportunity cost being the determinant of the going price observed. It is marginalism, which in non-Austrian versions is expressed by the production function and its partial derivatives—not by the deeper idea in Austrian economics, and humanomics, of expectations of subjective value. Of course the expectations of the various owners differ, as is evident in the willingness of one to sell out to another. He declares that "we must not abstract from those acts of the mind in choice *and interpretation* that shape and constitute the social world."[10] A little later in the same essay he asserts that the neo-Ricardians "admit with a bad conscience" this idea of interpretation and that "the neoclassicals [actually, the Samuelsonians] have to ignore it entirely, since their formal apparatus [namely, the book of routine blueprints that Samuelson offered as a metaphor for the production function] offers no scope for the interpretive action of the human mind."[11] Of the devotees of the neoclassical synthesis of 1900, which bypassed the Austrian neoclassicals, he writes, "The individual interests them only in his capacity as a possessor of given tastes, not as a possessor of a mind capable of probing and digesting experience, of acquiring and diffusing knowledge," or having differing subjective values of capital goods.[12]

That is what economics needs, as the field of psychology did acquire in the 1960s, if imperfectly—a theory of a human mind. (Psychologists have since walked away from it and back to a version of behaviorism in neurology. The temptations of a snappy mechanism are great.) Lachmann can lead us to it and to a full humanomics. It extends (but also to some degree calls into question) modern economics and the numerous other social sciences from law to sociology now influenced by an exclusively Max U and materialist economics.

PART II
The Killer App

The Killer App of Humanomics Is the Evidence That the Great Enrichment Came from Ethics and Rhetoric

At the annual meeting of the American Economic Association in San Diego in 2004, I gave a highly tentative talk on what I had not yet learned to call humanomics, in that case the bringing of serious ethical reflection into the history and economics of commercially tested betterment. In the Q and A Herb Gintis stood up and suggested amiably, "I see what you mean, Deirdre. But you need a killer app, an explanation of an important economic event that shows that the humanities matter."

Thanks for the comment, Herb. Here it is. If you want more evidence, consult the trilogy on the Bourgeois Era. Or at least buy it.

*   *   *

From 1800 to the present the average person on the planet has been enriched in real terms, I have noted, by a factor of about ten, or to be arithmetically precise by some 900 percent. Call it 1,000 percent, since we are dealing here with very rough figures: 10 minus the base of 1 is the change, which divided by the base of 1 is 9, which multiplied by 100, to express it in percentage, is 900—or not to quibble about the arithmetic, 1,000 percent near enough. In the ever-rising share of places from Belgium to Botswana, and now China and India, that have agreed to the Bourgeois Deal—"Let me earn profits from creative destruction in the first act, and by the third act I will make all of *you* rich'"—the factor is thirty in conventional terms and, if one allows for improved quality of goods and services, such as improved glass and autos or improved medicine and higher education, a factor of one hundred. That is, the reward from allowing ordinary people to have a go, the rise at first in northwestern Europe and then worldwide of economic liberty and social dignity, eroding ancient hierarchy and evading modern regulation, has been anything from about 3,000 to about 10,000 percent. Previous "efflorescences," as the historical sociologist Jack Goldstone calls them, such as the glory of Greece or the boom of Song China, and indeed the Industrial Revolution of the eighteenth century in Britain, resulted perhaps in doublings or at the most triplings of real income per person—100 or 200 percent, as against fully 3,000 percent since 1800 and higher. The French classicist Alain Bresson agrees with the British classicist Ian Morris, who examined archaeologically the size of houses, in putting the Greek factor of per capita increase from 750 BCE to 350 BCE at five or six.[1] According to Morris, the development of the wheat-oil-wine economy and its large extension in sea trade was the central cause of the enrichment. Bresson doubts the factor of increase is quite so high as five or six. But even if it were, admirable as such an efflorescence would be, it is 400 or 500 percent in four centuries, beside 3,000 or 10,000 percent of the Great Enrichment in two centuries.

What needs to be explained in a modern social science history is not the Industrial Revolution(s) but the Great Enrichment, one or two orders of magnitude larger than any previous change in human history. If we are going to be seriously quantitative and scientific and social and economic, we need to stop obsessing about, say, whether Europe experienced a doubling or a tripling of real income over the many centuries before 1800 or about this or that expansion of trade in coal or iron. We need to take seriously the lesson of comparative history that Europe was *not* special until 1700 or so. We need to explain the largest social and economic change since the invention of agriculture, which is not the Industrial Revolution—not to mention lesser efflorescences such as the Song Dynasty or the Quattrocento—but the Great Enrichment of our day and now our world.

In explaining it, I argued at insane length in the trilogy (but insane length is perhaps what so important a question requires) using quantitative and qualitative evidence, it will not do to focus on capital accumulation or hierarchical exploitation, on trade expansion or class struggle. This is for two sorts of reasons, the first historical and the second economic. (I do not expect you here to agree instantly with any of these. I list some of them here only as placeholders and invite you to examine the full marshalling of the evidence. Here I mean only to gesture toward the issues involved.)

Historically speaking, neither accumulation nor exploitation nor trade nor struggle is unique to the early modern world. Medieval peasants in Europe saved more, in view of their miserable yield-seed ratios, than did any eighteenth-century bourgeois.[2] Slave societies such as those of the classical Mediterranean could in peaceful times see a doubling of real income per person or maybe even Morris's perhaps exaggerated factor of five or six, but no 3,000 percent explosion of ingenuity such as overcame northwestern Europe after 1800. As to trade as an engine of growth, the largest sea trade until very late was across the Indian Ocean, not the Atlantic, yet it yielded no signs of a Great Enrichment among its participants. As to struggle, unionism and worker-friendly regulation came only after the Great Enrichment was well under way, not before. Thus, world history.

Economically speaking, capital accumulation runs out of steam (even literally) in a few decades. As Keynes wrote in 1936, the savings rate in the absence of innovation will deprive "capital of its scarcity-value within one or two generations."[3] Taking by exploitation from slaves or workers will result merely in more such capital accumulation, if it does, as Marx said, and for that reason faces the same diminishing returns. And exploitation of, say, British workers is anyway unable to explain a Great Enrichment that enriched even the exploited, absent a massive innovation that is unexplained in the story of surplus value. The gains from trade, to look at the political right's favorite, are good to have, but Harberger triangles show that they are small when put on the scale of a 10,000 percent enrichment, or even 3,000 or 1,000 percent. Government regulation, to turn back to the left's explanations, works by reducing the gains from commercially tested betterment. It's hard to see how it could account for a factor of thirty. And unions work mainly by shifting income from one part of the working class to another, as from sick people and apartment renters to doctors and plumbers. Thus, modern economics.

What then?

This. What explains the Great Enrichment is not material but a novel liberty and dignity for ordinary people, among them the innovating bourgeoisie. In a word, it was the first, modest moves toward social and economic and political *liberalism*, Adam Smith's "obvious and simple plan of natural liberty."[4] It gave masses of ordinary people—such as the chandler's apprentice Benjamin Franklin or the wigmaker Richard Arkwright or the boy telegrapher Thomas Edison—an opportunity to have a go, testing their ideas in commerce. Neither capital nor institutions, which were secondary and dependent, initiated our riches. It was the articulated idea of human equality that did it. Ideas show in speech and letters and literature, and are studied by the humanities, the tools of which therefore are highly relevant for understanding the Great Enrichment. Egalitarian economic and social ideas, not in the first instance steam engines and universities, made the modern world.

"One history of Western politics," writes the political philosopher Mika LaVaque-Manty, citing Charles Taylor and Peter Berger (he could have cited most European writers on the matter from Locke and Voltaire and Wollstonecraft through Tocqueville and Arendt and Rawls),

> has it that under modernity, equal dignity has replaced positional honor as the ground on which individuals' political status rests: Now, the story goes, the dignity which I have by virtue of nothing more than my humanity gives me both standing as a citizen vis-à-vis the state and a claim to respect from others. Earlier, my political status would have depended, first, on who I was (more respect for the well-born, less for the lower orders) and also on how well I acquitted myself as that sort of person. In rough outline, the story is correct.[5]

Article 3 of the Italian Constitution adopted in 1948 (the constitution was later much revised, but not in this article) is typical: "All the citizens have equal social dignity and are equal before the law, without distinctions of sex, of race, of language, of religion, of political opinion, of personal and social position."[6]

"But," LaVaque-Manty continues, "there are important complications to it." One important complication is that Europeans used their older and existing values to argue for new ones. Humans do. LaVaque-Manty observes that "aristocratic social practices and values themselves get used to ground and shape modernity." He argues that the strange egalitarianism of early modern dueling with swords or pistols by *non*aristocrats, such as Burr and Hamilton, was a case in point.[7] Likewise, in 1877 a wholesale merchant in Ibsen's *Pillars of Society* clinches a deal by reference to his (noble) Viking ancestors: "It's settled, Bernick! A Norseman's word stands firm as a rock, you know that!"[8] An American businessman will use the myth of the cowboy for similar assurances. Likewise, Christian social practices and values got used to ground and shape modernity, such as the amplification of Abrahamic individualism before God, then the social gospel and Catholic social teaching, then socialism out of religious doctrines of charity, and then environmentalism out of religious doctrines of stewardship. European intellectual practices and values in the medieval universities (imitated from the Islamic world) and in the royal societies of the seventeenth century—and again in the Humboldtian modern university after 1810—were based on traditional principles of intellectual hierarchy. But they then get used to raise the dignity of any arguer. Witness the blogosphere.

The uniquely (for a while) European ideas of individual liberty for all free men—and at length, startlingly (and to the continuing distress of some conservatives), for slaves and women and young people and sexual minorities and handicapped people and immigrants—was generalized from much older bourgeois liberties granted town by town. The principle was to give to every other human being every right that you claim for yourself. Such was not the doctrine of many other people even in the late eighteenth century. Now it is universal, at any rate in declaration. The universality inspirits ordinary people, bringing a mass of folk to commercially tested betterments of their own devising. Douglass North, John Wallis, and Barry Weingast, in their *Violence and Social Orders* (2009), interpret the transition from what they call "limited access" to "open access" societies as a shift from personal power for the Duke of Norfolk to impersonal power for Tom, Dick, and Harriet. The other word for it is *liberalism*. Think of the Magna Carta for all barons and the charters for all full citizens of a city, and finally "all men are created equal."

The doctrinal change might have happened earlier, and in other parts of the world, and persisted as the liberal idea has since the eighteenth century. But it didn't. The Athenian state in the age of Pericles was imagined to be perpetually lived, and its empire had surely exhibited its monopoly of (naval) violence. Justice was given to all, except perhaps those troublesome slaves, women, allies, and foreigners. Pericles in his Funeral Oration said of Athens, "we are called a democracy, for the administration is in the hands of the many and not of the few. . . . There exists equal justice to all [free male citizens] and alike in their private disputes. . . . Neither is poverty an obstacle, but a [free] man may benefit his country whatever the obscurity of his condition."[9] Democracy is equality before the law and further, as Pericles and Alexis de Tocqueville and I would add, equality of *dignity*, such as Tocqueville noted in the lack of deference to social superiors in 1830s America. Liberalism. Alfeed Reckendrees pointed out that liberalism characterized Weimar Germany, but it failed, as he argues, for lack of ethics. Not matter, but ideas. So did Athenian democracy when, as Thucydides put it, ethical "words [such as justice] lost their meaning," and as Tocqueville worried about in the rule of mobs, now revived in anti-immigrant populism.[10]

In a recent collective history of "capitalism," one of the editors, Larry Neal, offers a neoinstitutionalist definition of the word as (1) private property rights, (2) contracts enforceable by third parties, (3) markets with responsive prices, and (4) supportive governments.[11] He does not appear to realize that the first three conditions have applied to almost every human society. They can be found in pre-Columbian Mayan marketplaces and Aboriginal trade gatherings, in the Icelandic Althing in the tenth century CE and the leaders of Israel ("judges") in the twelfth century BCE. "Capitalism" in this sense did not "rise."

The fourth condition, "supportive governments," is precisely the doctrinal change to laissez-faire and social dignity and to a slowly implemented liberalism unique to northwestern Europe. What did rise as a result of liberty and dignity was not trade itself but commercially tested *betterment* once the mass of people could have a go. The idea of equality of liberty and dignity for all humans, though imperfectly realized and a continuing project down to the present, caused and then protected a startling material and then spiritual progress. What was crucial in Europe and its offshoots was the new economic liberty and social dignity for the swelling bourgeois segment of commoners, encouraged after 1700 in England and especially after 1800 on a wider scale to perform massive betterments, the discovery of new ways tested by increasingly freed trade.

Thus, the killer app of humanistic learning. Herb hasn't told me if he's satisfied yet.

CHAPTER TEN

The Dignity of Liberalism Did It

The idea of universal dignity—the social honoring of all people, the idea of liberalism exhibited in novels and plays, political philosophy and political declarations—was necessary and sufficient when bundled with liberty in encouraging people to enter new trades and to protect their economic liberty to do so.

A testing countercase is European Jewry down to 1945, gradually liberated to have a go in Holland in the seventeenth century and Britain in the eighteenth century and Germany and the rest later. Legally speaking, by 1900 from Ireland to the Austrian Empire any Jew could enter any profession, take up any innovative idea. But in many parts of Europe he was never granted the other, sociological half of the encouragement to betterment, the dignity that protects the liberty. "Society, confronted with political, economic, and legal equality for Jews," wrote Hannah Arendt, "made it quite clear that none of its classes was prepared to grant them social equality. . . . Social pariahs the Jews did become wherever they had ceased to be political and civil outcasts."[1] True, Benjamin Disraeli became prime minister of the United Kingdom in 1868, Lewis Wormeer Harris was elected Lord Mayor of Dublin in 1876, and Louis Brandeis became an associate justice of the US Supreme Court in 1916. Yet in Germany after 1933 few gentile doctors or professors resisted the expulsion of Jews from their ranks. The Jews were undignified. In much of Christendom—with partial exceptions in the United States and the United Kingdom, and in Denmark and Bulgaria—Jews were political and social outcasts.

Liberty and dignity for all commoners, to be sure, was a double-sided political and social ideal. History has many cunning passages, contrived corridors. The liberty of the bourgeoisie to venture was matched by the liberty of the workers, when they got the vote, to adopt growth-killing regulations with a socialist clerisy cheering them on. And the dignity of workers was overmatched by an arrogance among successful entrepreneurs and wealthy rentiers with a fascist clerisy cheering them on. Such are the inevitable tensions of liberal democracy. And such are the often mischievous dogmas of the clerisy.

But for the first time, thank God—and thank the English Levellers and then Locke in the seventeenth century and then Voltaire and Smith and Franklin and Paine and Wollstonecraft, among other advanced thinkers in the eighteenth century—the ordinary people, the commoners, both workers and bosses, began to be released from the ancient notion of hierarchy, the naturalization of the noble gentleman's rule over hoi polloi. Aristotle had said that most people were born to be slaves. "From the hour of their birth, some are marked out for subjection, others for rule."[2] Bishop (and Saint) Isidore of Seville said in the early seventh century that '"to those unsuitable for liberty, [God] has mercifully accorded servitude."[3] So it had been from the first times of settled agriculture and the ownership of land. Inherited wealth was long thought blameless compared with wealth earned by work, about which suspicion hung.[4] Consider South Asia with its ancient castes, the hardest workers at the bottom. And farther east consider the Confucian tradition (if not in every detail the ideas of Kung the Teacher himself), which stressed the Five Relationships of ruler to subject, father to son, husband to wife, elder brother to younger, and—the only one of the five without hierarchy—friend to friend.

The analogy of the king as father of the nation, and therefore "naturally" superior, ruled political thought in the West (and the East and North and South) right through Thomas Hobbes. King Charles I of England, of whom Hobbes approved, was articulating nothing but a universal and ancient notion when he declared in his speech from the scaffold in 1649 that "a subject and a sovereign are plain different things."[5] But the analogy of natural fathers to natural kings and aristocracies commenced about then, gradually, to seem less obvious to some of the bolder thinkers. The Leveller Richard Rumbold on his own scaffold in 1685 declared, "I am sure there was no man born marked of God above another; for none comes into the world with a saddle on his back, neither any booted and spurred to ride him."[6] Few in the crowd gathered to mock him would have agreed. A century later, many would have. By 1985 virtually everyone did.

True, outpourings of egalitarian sentiment, such as that by Jesus of Nazareth around 30 CE ("Inasmuch as ye have done it unto one of the least of these my brethren, ye have done it unto me" [Matt. 25:40]), had shaken all agricultural societies from time to time. But from the seventeenth century onward the shaking became continuous, and then down to the present became a rolling earthquake of equality for all humans. Praise God.

In the nineteenth century in Europe (if not yet in Bollywood) the ancient comic plot of young lovers amusingly fooling the Old Man, or being tragically stymied by him, died out, because human capital embodied in and owned by young people replaced in economic dominance the landed capital owned by the old. Even patriarchy, therefore, the sovereignty of fathers, began to tremble until nowadays most American and Scandinavian children defy their fathers with impunity. Four verses before the verse in Leviticus routinely hauled out to damn homosexuals, their putative author Moses commands that "every one that curseth his father or his mother shall surely be put to death" (Lev. 20:9). The verse would condemn most teenagers in liberal countries to stoning, along with the homosexuals and those who mix wool cloth with linen or fail to take a ceremonial bath after their periods.

In its long, laborious development, the loony notion of dignity for anyone coming into the world without a saddle on his back was taken up by radical Anabaptists and Quakers, abolitionists and spiritualists, revolutionaries and suffragettes, and the American drag queens battling the cops at Stonewall. By now in free countries the burden of proof has shifted decisively onto conservatives and party hacks and Catholic bishops and country-club Colonel Blimps and anti-1960s reactionaries to defend hierarchy, the generous loyalty to rank and sex, as a thing lovely and in accord with natural law.

The Rumboldian idea of coming into the world without a saddle on one's back had expressed, too, a notion struggling for legitimacy, of a contract between king and people. As Rumbold put it in his speech, "the king having, as I conceive, power enough to make him great; the people also as much property as to make them happy; they being, as it were, contracted to one another."[7] Note the "as it were, contracted," a Bourgeois Deal akin to Abram's land deal with the Lord, a Jewish rhetoric of "covenant" popular after Zwingli among Protestants. The terms of such a monarchical deal became a routine trope in the seventeenth century, as in Hobbes and Locke, and then still more routinely in the eighteenth century. Louis XIV declared that he was tied to his subjects "only by an exchange of reciprocal obligations. The deference . . . we receive . . . [is] but payment for the justice [the subjects] expect to receive."[8] And Frederick the Great claimed to view himself as governed by a similar deal with his subjects, calling himself merely "the first servant of the state" (though not refraining from exercising autocracy when he felt like it).

Even in autocratic France and Prussia (if not in Russia), the sovereign had to honor property rights. It is not true that private property and the rule of law was born in 1688. Thus, the liberty half of liberty and dignity. In the Putney Debates in 1647, Richard Overton had declared that "by natural birth all men are equally and alike born to like propriety [that is, equal rights to acquire and hold property], liberty and freedom."[9] The deal by which the people as a group had as much property as to make them "happy" (a new concern in the late seventeenth century, at any rate compared with medieval notions of aristocratic dignity and clerical holiness) was thought crucial among a handful of such progressives and then by more and more Europeans from the eighteenth century on. In the first French *Declaration of the Rights of Man and of the Citizen* in 1789, the last article (number 17) speaks of property in notably warm terms: "property is an inviolable and sacred right." Article 2 in the *Declaration* had placed property among four rights, "natural and imprescriptible": "liberty, property, security, and resistance to oppression."

An article in the Universal Declaration of Human Rights adopted by the United Nations in 1948 (by God's little joke, also numbered 17) declares (though in a socialist-leaning age with rather less warmth than in 1789), "(1) Everyone has the right to own property alone as well as in association with others; and (2) No one shall be arbitrarily deprived of his property." Article 42 in the new Italian Constitution, in force in the same year, is still less warm: "Private property is recognized and guaranteed by the law, which prescribes the ways it is acquired, enjoyed and its limitations so as to ensure its social function and make it accessible to all. In the cases provided for by the law and with provisions for compensation, private property may be expropriated for reasons of general interest." The socialist tilt toward "social function," "accessib[ility] to all," and a "general interest" that could justify expropriation was lively in the twentieth century. In 1986 the Labor prime minister of Australia, Bob Hawke, proposed for his country a Bill of Rights. It made no mention of the right to property.[10]

In the twentieth century the rhetorical presumption of life, liberty, and the pursuit of happiness for all was echoed even in the rhetoric of its most determined enemies (as in "the Democratic People's Republic of North Korea" and other communist/fascist countries in which democracy and the people are in fact spurned). The collectivist counterdeal by which such regimes actually worked, born with Rousseau, was that the general will would be discerned by the party or the führer. No need for private property, then. We in government will take care of all that, thanks.

Democratic pluralism, I noted, was double sided. Progressive redistributions, under the theories of Rousseau and Proudhon that property is anyway theft, killed betterment. Consider Argentina, joined recently by Venezuela. Such cases bring to mind the American journalist H. L. Mencken's grim witticism in 1916 that democracy is "the theory that the common people know what they want and deserve to get it, good and hard."[11] He also said "Democracy is the art and science of running the circus from the monkey cage."[12] Yet on the other side of the balance, a populist commitment to modest redistribution—though understand that most benefits, such as free higher education, go to the voting middle class, just as minimum wages protect middle-class trade unionists and are paid in substantial part to the children of the middle class working at the local bar—saved social-democratic countries from the chaos of revolution. Think of postwar Germany, or for that matter the American New Deal.[13]

What came under question in the world from 1517 to 1848 and beyond, slowly, on account of the religious radicals of the sixteenth century and then the political radicals of the seventeenth and eighteenth centuries and then the abolitionist and black and feminist and gay and untouchable radicals of the nineteenth and twentieth centuries, was the ancient lack of liberty and lack of dignity, the one political, the other social. The questioning had dramatic consequences in encouraging commercially tested betterment. The English Levellers of the 1640s, who were not modern property-hating socialists, had demanded free trade. They were in this, by the standards of the time, terrifying innovators, as in manhood suffrage and annual parliaments.

What made us free and rich was the questioning of the notion that "a liberty" was a special privilege accorded to a guildsman of the town or to a nobleman of the robe and the supporting notion that the only "dignity" was privilege inherited from such men and their charter-granting feudal lords, or graciously subgranted by them to you, their humble servant down below in the great chain of being. The evidence is to be found in the history, philosophy, literature, and talk of the times. Not in prices and incomes, trade flows and class interests alone. Philip the Good, duke of the Burgundian Netherlands, forced in 1438 the proud city of Bruges to accede to his rising power. His tyranny took the form of taking away its special "privileges." But his granddaughter, Mary, Duchess of Burgundy, was forced to sign the Groot Privilege, the bourgeois Magna Carta of the Low Countries, giving such liberties back to all of the cities. Equality before the law.

It was not only dukes and duchesses who took, or granted, privileges denied to most people. *Homo hierarchus* reappears. Hierarchy was reworked by the bourgeoisie itself into commercial forms, even in the first northern home of bourgeois glory. A famous radical poem of the Netherlands in the 1930s, written on a slow news day by Jan Gresshof (he was fired for printing the poem in the newspaper he edited), speaks of the conservative wing of the bourgeois clerisy, "*de dominee, de dokter, de notaris*" (the minister, the doctor, the lawyer-notary), who together strolled complacently on Arnhem's town square of an evening. "There is nothing left on earth for them to learn, / They are perfect and complete, / Old liberals [in the European sense], distrustful and healthy."[14] The hierarchy now to be broken down was of the members of the bourgeoisie itself remade as pseudo-neokings and neoknights when they could get away with it. Thus a trophy wife in Florida clinging to the arm of her rich husband declared to the television cameras, on the subject of poor people, "We don't bother with *losers*." Thus the Medici (as their name implies) started as doctors by way of routinely learned skills, then became bankers by entrepreneurship, and then grand dukes by violence, and at last kept their dukedom by the settled hierarchy of inheritance and the legitimate monopoly of coercion.

The economic historian Joel Mokyr has noted that the Dutch became in the eighteenth-century conservative and "played third fiddle in the Industrial Revolution," from which he concludes that there must be something amiss in McCloskey's emphasis on the new ideology of bourgeois liberty and dignity.[15] After all, the Dutch had them both, early. But I just said that the bourgeoisie is capable of reversing its betterment by imposing its own honorable hierarchy, which is what the Dutch regents did. And Mokyr is adopting the mistaken convention that the Dutch in the eighteenth century "failed." They did not. Like Londoners, and according to comparative advantage, they gave up some of their own industrial projects in favor of becoming bankers and routine merchants. I am claiming only that the new ideology came to Britain from the Netherlands with King William in the 1690s, which remains true whether or not the Dutch did much with it later. In their earlier, Golden Age, the Dutch with their liberal ideology certainly did a lot of bettering. I agree that Dutch society later froze up, ruled by *de dominee, de dokter, de notaris*. But national borders do not compute. If we are to blame the Dutch in the eighteenth century for conservatism, we will also have to blame the Southern English, who also turned to specializing in mere trading and financing, giving up their industrial might, clipping coupons in the funds and sitting in great houses surrounded by parkland, and, like the Dutch, adhering to distinctions of rank that were less important in the industrial north of England or in the industrial south of Belgium.

And Mokyr uses an unspoken lemma of inertia—that once initiated, a social change must be permanent (or else it did not exist in the first place, which is how Mokyr argues that the liberal ideological thrust to innovism in the Low Countries was not as important as science). The lemma raises graver problems for his own emphasis on the new science and the Republic of Letters as the initiating events than for my emphasis on a new appreciation for bourgeois liberty and dignity (which then, by the way, mightily encouraged science and the Republic of Letters). After all, the Dutch in the seventeenth century had invented the telescope and the microscope among numerous other scientific devices, such as the pendulum clock. Why did not inertia propel them, if science does it, into the Industrial Revolution and the Great Enrichment? The Dutch case argues better for bourgeois dignity, which has sustained the Netherlands ever since as one of the richest countries in the world. It argues poorly for science, in which it did falter.

The ethical and rhetorical change that around 1700 began to break the ancient restraints on betterment, whether from the old knights or the new monopolists, was liberating, and it was enlightened, and it was liberal (in the Scottish sense of putting first an equal liberty of permission for people, not a Rousseauian sense of equal riches in outcome). And it was successful. As one of its more charming conservative enemies put it:

> Locke sank into a swoon;
> The Garden died;
> God took the spinning-jenny
> Out of his side.[16]

CHAPTER ELEVEN

Ideas, Not Incentives, Underlie It

It is merely a materialist-economistic prejudice to insist on the contrary that such a rhetorical change from aristocratic-religious values to bourgeois values and especially the widespread social and political *approval* of bourgeois values—what I call the Bourgeois Revaluation—*must* have had economic or biological roots. John Mueller, a political scientist and historian at Ohio State University, argues that war, like slavery or the subordination of women, has become slowly less respectable in the past few centuries.[1] Important habits of the heart and of the lip do change, the way Athens became democratic or Rome Christian or north Germany Protestant. In the seventeenth century a master could routinely beat his servant. Not now. Such changes are not *always* caused by interest or by considerations of efficiency or by the logic of class conflict or by the adventures of Max U. The Bourgeois Revaluation had also legal, political, personal, gender, religious, philosophical, historical, linguistic, journalistic, literary, artistic, and accidental causes. To understand it one must study them too.

The economist Deepak Lal, relying on the legal historian Harold Berman and echoing an old opinion of Henry Adams, sees a big change in the eleventh century in Gregory VII's assertion of church supremacy.[2] Perhaps. I am not eager to speak against ideational explanations such as Lal's even though they are not exactly mine. At least he's not depending on an unthinking materialism. But the trouble with such earlier and broader origins, such as equality before God in Abrahamic religions or Gregory's battle, is that modernity came from Holland and England, not, for example, from thoroughly Protestant Sweden or East Prussia (except from ur-modern Kant) or from thoroughly church-supremacist Spain or Naples (except from

ur-modern Vico). It is better to locate the widespread taking up of the politically relevant attitudes later in European history—around 1700. Such a
dating fits better with the historical finding that until the eighteenth century
places like China, say, did not look markedly less rich or even, in many respects, less free than Europe.[3] In Europe the scene was set by the affirma-
tions of ordinary life, and ordinary death, in the upheavals of the Reformation of the sixteenth century, the long civil war between French Catholics and
Huguenots (1562–1598), the longer Dutch revolt against Spain (1568–1648),
and in the seventeenth century the English revolutions (1642–1651, 1688–
1689). The economically relevant change in attitude that resulted occurred
in the late seventeenth and early eighteenth centuries with the novel ruminations around the North Sea—embodied literally in the novel as against the
romance—affirming as the transcendent telos of an economy an ordinary
instead of a heroic or holy life. Look in 1719 at *Robinson Crusoe*. Look in
1749 at *Tom Jones, A Foundling*. It was, in one of the philosopher Charles
Taylor's labels for it, "the sanctification of ordinary life."[4]

Margaret Jacob, the historian of technology and of the Radical Enlightenment (her pioneering coinage), argues persuasively that the 1680s were
the hinge. The Anglo-Dutch reaction to absolutism was the "catalyst for
what we call Enlightenment."[5] Enlightenment comes, she is saying, from
the reaction to a Catholic absolutism in England secretly encouraged by
Charles II and openly encouraged by his brother James II and in France
at the time under Louis XIV with the Revocation of the Edict of Nantes
(1685) and Louis's secret offers of help for Charles and James. Jack Goldstone observes that in England in the 1680s, even the common law was
under attack, exhibited in the trial and execution of Richard Rumbold.
In other words, it was the politics, not economic materialism, that started
what Mokyr calls the Industrial Enlightenment. After all, absolutist and
Catholic France and antiabsolutist and Protestant England were both of
them mercantilist. It's not mercantilism, then. And the Dutch, French,
and English, not to speak of the Portuguese and Spanish, had long been
imperialists. It's not imperialism, then. What changed were political and
social ideas—not economic interests.

The common set of ideas in the Enlightenment were ethical and political. For example, it came to be said (if by no means always done) that one
must settle matters by making open arguments, not by applying political force. The "new" meta-idea was Erasmian humanism and the ancient
tradition of rhetoric. The Reformation finally evolved in an Erasmian
direction, though only after rivers of blood had been spilt in the name

of "whose reign it is, his religion holds." And out of the Radical Reformation's idea of nonhierarchical church governance, the advanced thinking became even democratic, after more blood had been spilt. The ideas were European, from Scotland to Poland, but most forward in the tumultuous northwestern edge of the place. Without such ideas, the modern world might possibly have happened in Europe after a while, but in a different way—a centralized, French version, say. It would not have worked so well economically (though the cuisine would have been better).

The aristocracy had said that they disdained the dishonor of merely economic trade and betterment. The Medici bank lasted only about a century because its later governors were more interested in hobnobbing with the old aristocracy than in making sensible loans to merchants.[6] The scholastic intellectuals, for all their admirable rhetorical seriousness, did not get their hands dirty in experimentation (with rare exceptions such as Roger Bacon, who was imprisoned for his pains). It was sixteenth-century Dutch and English merchants, following on their earlier merchant cousins in the Mediterranean, who developed the notion of the experimental and observing life.[7] Enlightenment was a change in the attitude toward such ordinary life. The rare honor of kings and dukes and bishops was to be devalued. And such honor was to be extended to merchant bankers of London and to American experimenters with electricity. The comparative devaluation of courts and politics followed, slowly.

By the middle of the eighteenth century, the debate, as the political theorist and intellectual historian John Danford notes, was "whether a free society is possible if commercial activities flourish."[8] The admired models on the anticommercial side of the debate, as J. G. A. Pocock and others have shown, were Republican Rome and especially, of all places, Greek Sparta. The vulgar commerce favored by Athens or Carthage or now Britain would introduce "luxury and voluptuousness," in Lord Kames's conventional phrase, as the debate reached its climax, which would "eradicate patriotism" and extinguish at least ancient freedom, the freedom to participate. As the Spartans vanquished Athens, so, too, some more vigorous nation would rise up and vanquish Britain, or at any rate stop a "progress so flourishing . . . when patriotism is the ruling passion of every member."[9] One hears such arguments still, in nostalgic praise in the United States for the Greatest Generation (lynching, police beating, and an income in today's dollars, ca. 1945, a quarter of what it became later) as against the diminished glory of our latter days (civil rights, boards of civilian review of the police, and income per head at least four times higher, and much higher in quality). The nationalist, sacrificial, antiluxury, classical republican view with its Spartan ideal persists in the United States in the pages of the *Nation* and the *National Review*, with European parallels.

On the contrary, said Hume, in reply to arguments such as Kames's, commerce is good for us. Georgian mercantilism and overseas imperialism in aid of the political, he said, was *not* good for us. Hume opposed, writes Danford, "the primacy of the political."[10] "In this denigration of political life Hume [is] thoroughly modern and [seems] to agree in important respects with [the individualism of] Hobbes and Locke." Hobbes, Danford argues, believed that the tranquility notably lacking in the Europe of his time could best be achieved "if the political order [is] understood as merely a means to security and prosperity rather than virtue (or salvation or empire)."[11] "This amounts," Danford notes, "to an enormous demotion of politics," now to be seen as merely instrumental as against an arena for the exercise of the highest virtues of a tiny group of The Best.[12] We nowadays can't easily see how novel such a demotion was because we now suppose, without a sense of its historical oddness, that to secure these rights, governments are instituted among men, deriving their just powers from the consent of the governed. Politics has stopped being exclusively the plaything of the aristocracy, lethal games in Wolf Hall.

Hume spoke of the "opposition between the greatness of the state and the happiness of the subjects."[13] In an earlier time Machiavelli could easily adopt the greatness of the Prince as the purpose of a polity, at any rate when he was angling for a job with the Medici princes. The purpose of Sparta was not the "happiness" of the Spartan women, helots, allies, or even in any material sense the Spartanate itself. "Go tell the Spartans, stranger passing by, / That here obedient to their laws we lie." The entire point of Henry VIII's England was Henry's glory as by the Grace of God, King of England, France and Ireland, Defender of the Faith and of the Church of England and in Earth Supreme Head.

To devalue thus royal or aristocratic values is to leave the bourgeoisie in charge. It happened in Holland. Romantic people, attached on the political right to king and country and on the political left to revolution, sneer at the Enlightenment, then and now.[14] What was unique about the Enlightenment was precisely the elevation of ordinary, peaceful people in ordinary, peaceful life, an elevation of trade over the monopoly of coercion.

* * *

The Swedish political scientist Erik Ringmar's answer to the question why was Europe first begins from the simple and true triad of points that

(1) all change involves an initial reflection (namely, that change is possible), (2) an entrepreneurial moment (putting the change into practice), and (3) "pluralism" or "toleration." I would rather call the toleration the "ideology of the Bourgeois Era," namely, the Bourgeois Revaluation—some way of counteracting the annoyance with which the naturally conservative majority of humans will view any moving of their cheese. "Contemporary Britain, the United States or Japan," Ringmar writes, "are not modern because they contain individuals who are uniquely reflective, entrepreneurial or tolerant."[15] That's correct: the psychological hypothesis one finds in Weber or in the psychologist David McClelland or in the historian David Landes does not stand up to the evidence, as for example the success of the overseas Chinese or indeed the astonishingly quick turn from Maoist starvation in mainland China to 10 percent rates of growth per year per person or from the Hindu rate of growth and the License Raj in India after independence to growth rates per person since 1991 over 6 percent. Why would mass psychology change so quickly? And how could a rise of an entrepreneurial spirit from, say, 5 percent of the population to 10 percent, which could have also characterized earlier efflorescences such as fifth-century Athens, cause after 1800 a uniquely Great Enrichment of a factor of thirty?

But then unhappily Ringmar contends in Douglass North style, "A modern society is a society in which change happens automatically and effortlessly because it is institutionalized."[16] The trouble with the claim of "institutions" is, as Ringmar himself notes earlier in another connection, that "it begs the question of the origin."[17] It also begs the question of enforcement, which depends on ethics and opinion absent from the neoinstitutionalist tale. "The joker in the pack," writes the economic historian Eric Jones in speaking of the decline of guild restrictions in England, "was the national shift in elite opinion, which the courts partly shared":

> The judges often declined to support the restrictiveness that the guilds sought to impose. . . . As early as the start of seventeenth century, towns had been losing cases they took to court with the aim of compelling new arrivals to join their craft guilds. . . . A key case concerned Newbury and Ipswich in 1616. The ruling in this instance became a common law precedent, to the effect that "foreigners", men from outside a borough, could not be compelled to enrol.[18]

Ringmar devotes 150 lucid and learned and literate pages to exploring the origins of European science, humanism, newspapers, universities, academies, theater, novels, corporations, property rights, insurance, Dutch finance, diversity, states, politeness, civil rights, political parties, and economics. But he is a true comparativist (he taught for some years in China)—this in sharp contrast to some of the other Northians, and especially the good, much missed Douglass North himself. So Ringmar does not suppose that the European facts speak for themselves. In the following one hundred even better pages he takes back much of the implicit claim that Europe was anciently special, whether "institutionalized" or not, by going through for China the same triad of reflection, entrepreneurship, and pluralism/toleration and finding them pretty good. "The Chinese were at least as intrepid [in the seas] as the Europeans"; "the [Chinese] imperial state constituted next to no threat to the property rights of merchants and investors"; "already by 400 BCE China produced as much cast iron as Europe would in 1750"; Confucianism was "a wonderfully flexible doctrine"; "China was far more thoroughly commercialized"; European "salons and coffee shops [were] . . . in some ways strikingly Chinese."[19] He knows, as the Northians appear not to, that China had banks and canals and large and specialized firms and private property many centuries before the Northian date for the acquisition of such modernities in England—the end of the seventeenth century.

The economist and historian Sheilagh Ogilvie criticizes the neoinstitutionalists and their claims that efficiency ruled, arguing on the contrary for a "conflictual" point of view in which power is taken seriously:

> Efficiency theorists do sometimes mention that institutions evoke conflict. But they seldom incorporate conflict into their explanations. Instead, conflict remains an incidental by-product of institutions portrayed as primarily existing to enhance efficiency. . . . Although serfdom [for example] was profoundly ineffective at increasing the size of the economic pie, it was highly effective at distributing large slices to overlords, with fiscal and military side-benefits to rulers and economic privileges for serf elites.[20]

The same can be said for the new political and social ideas that at length broke down an ideology that had been highly effective at justifying in ethical terms the distribution of large slices to overlords.

Why, then, a change in a system so profitable for the elite? Ringmar again gets it right again when he speaks of public opinion, which was a late and contingent development in Europe and to which he recurs frequently.[21] The oldest newspaper still publishing in Europe is a Swedish one of 1645, *Post- och Inrikes Tidningar* (Foreign and domestic times), and the first daily one in England dates to 1702. Benjamin Franklin's older brother James quickly imitated in Boston in 1721 the idea of a newspaper and became, with the active help of adolescent Ben, a thorn in the side of the authorities. That is, the institutions that mattered the most were not the "incentives" beloved of the economists, such as patents of invention (which have been shown to be insignificant, and anyway have been universal, as state-granted monopolies, from the first formation of states) or property rights (which were established and protected in China and India and the Ottoman Empire, often much earlier than in Europe, and after all in Europe the Roman law was clear enough on property). The important "institutions" were ideas, words, rhetoric, ideology. And these did change on the eve of the Great Enrichment. What changed circa 1700 was a climate of persuasion, which led promptly in Ringmar's terms to the amazing reflection, entrepreneurship, and pluralism called the modern world.

It is not always true, as Ringmar claims at one point, that "institutions are best explained in terms of the path through which they developed."[22] He contradicts himself on the page previous and there speaks truth: often "the institutions develop first and the needs come only later." It is not the case for example that the origins of English betterment are usefully traced to early medieval times. It is not the case that, say, English common law was essential for modernity. The historian David Le Bris has shown that before the Revolution, the French north *was* a common-law area while the south was a civil-law area but with little or no discernible differences in economic outcome during the next century.[23] Places without such law, further, promptly developed alternatives when the ideology turned, as it often did turn suddenly, in favor of betterment.

Why England? The evidence is massive that English rhetoric changed in favor of commercially tested betterment. In one of its aspects, it came out of the irritating successes of the Dutch. The successes of the Dutch Republic were startling to Europe. The English Navigation Acts and the three Anglo-Dutch Wars, by which in the middle of the seventeenth century England attempted in mercantilist and trade-is-war fashion to appropriate some Dutch success to itself, were the beginning of a larger English project of emulating the burghers of Delft and Leiden. "The evidence for this widespread envy of Dutch enterprise," wrote the historian Paul Kennedy in 1976, "is overwhelming."[24] Likewise the historian Matthew Kadane recently accounted for the English shift toward admiring the bourgeois virtues by "various interactions with the Dutch."[25] The English at the time put it in doggerel: "Make war with Dutchmen, peace with Spain / Then we shall have money and trade again." Yet it was not in fact warring against the Dutch that made England rich. Wars are expensive, and the Dutch *admiraals* Tromp and De Ruyter were no pushovers. It was imitating them that did the trick. Ideas. The Swedish historian Erik Thomson has shown that the English were not the only Europeans startled by the economic success of the United Provinces and ready, with some reluctance, to imitate them.[26]

Thomas Sprat, in his *History of the Royal Society* of 1667, attacked such envy and interaction and imitation. He viewed it as commendable that "the merchants of England live honorably in foreign parts" as quasi gentlemen, but "those of Holland meanly, minding their gain alone." Shameful. "Ours . . . [have] in their behavior very much the gentility of the families from which so many of them are descended [that is, the sending of younger sons into trade]. The others when they are abroad show that they are only a race of plain citizens," disgraceful "cits," as the antiurban sneer of the time had it. Perhaps it was, Sprat notes with annoyance, "one of the reasons they can so easily undersell us."[27] Possibly. John Dryden in 1672 took up Sprat's complaint in similar words. In his play *Amboyna; or, The Cruelties of the Dutch to the English Merchants*, the English merchant Beaumont addresses the Dutch: "For frugality in trading, we confess we cannot compare with you; for our merchants live like noblemen: your gentlemen, if you have any, live like boers," that is, low-class farmers.[28] Yet Josiah Child, arguing against guild regulation of cloth, admired the Dutch on nonaristocratic, prudential grounds: "if we intend to have the trade of the world we must imitate the Dutch."[29] Better boers we.

Ideas, not capital or institutions, made the modern world.

CHAPTER TWELVE

Even as to Time and Location

W hy indeed northwestern Europe? The answer is a case study in humanomics.

The causes were not racial or eugenic, a hardy tradition of scientific racism to the contrary (a scientific racism revived nowadays by some economists and evolutionary psychologists exhibiting a dismaying lack of understanding of the history of eugenics).[1] Nor was it English common law or an alleged "European individualism" or the traditions of the Germanic tribes in the Black Forest, as Romantic Europeans have been claiming now for two centuries.[2] "Culture can make all the difference," the historian David Landes used to say, by which he meant long-standing habits back to an ancient European superiority.[3] But it ain't so. That much is obvious, if the obviousness were not plain from the recent explosive economic successes of highly non-European and non-Germanic and even allegedly nonindividualistic places such as India and China, before them of Korea and Japan, and for a long time the economic successes of overseas versions of all kinds of ethnic groups, from Jews in North Africa to Parsees in England to Old Believers in Sydney.

Yet it is still an open question why China, for example, did not originate modern economic growth on the scale of the Great Enrichment—which by now you know I claim is one of the chief fruits of a liberal and bourgeois-admiring civilization. China had enormous cities and millions of merchants, and it had security of property and a gigantic free-trade area, when bourgeois northern Europeans were still hiding out in clusters of a very few thousand behind their tiny city walls and raising barriers to trade in all directions. Internal barriers to trade in China there were, but centrally and uniformly imposed, and nothing like the chaos of local tariffs, or measurements, or coins, in Europe. China had village schools and by early modern standards high rates of literacy and of numeracy. Until the fall of the Ming in 1644, it was highly literate compared to Europe. Chinese junks, gigantically larger than anything the Europeans could muster until the coming of iron hulls in the nineteenth century, were making occasional trips to the east coast of Africa before the Portuguese managed by a much shorter route to get there in their pathetic caravels. Yet the Portuguese, as the Chinese did not, persisted in sailing, naming for example the southeast African province of KwaZulu-Natal, far around the Cape of Good Hope, for the festival of Christ's Nativity of 1497 on which they first got there and inspiring other Europeans to a scramble for empire and trade, even in China itself. "We must sail," sang Luís de Camões, the Portuguese Virgil, in 1572. Gnaeus Pompey's ancient declaration that *Navigare necesse est; vivere non est necesse* (sailing is necessary; living is not) was adopted all over Europe—in Venice and Barcelona, then in Hamburg and Rotterdam. And so they did sail. No one else did, at least not with the loony passion of the Europeans in their mad search for luxury goods unavailable at home. And especially the technologically brilliant Chinese did not sail, except for their vigorous commerce with the Indian Ocean and Japan. If they had done so at a European level, North and South America would now be speaking a version of Cantonese.

Perhaps the problem was precisely China's unity, as against the ruck of Europe at the time: Genoa against Venice, Portugal against Spain, England against Holland, and even Rotterdam against Amsterdam. The Chinese and the other empires, such as the Moghuls and Ottomans, were rhetorically unified the way any large, one-boss organization thinks it is, such as a modern university. A "memorandum culture," such as Confucian China (or rather more paradoxically a modern university), has no space for rational discourse because the monarch does not *have* to pay attention.[4] Consider your local dean or provost, immune to reason in an institution allegedly devoted to reasoning. "Rational discussion is likely to flourish most," Barrington Moore has noted, "where it is least needed: where political [and religious] passions are minimal" (which would not describe the modern university).[5]

Jack Goldstone has noted that

China and India had great concentrations of capital in the hands of merchants; both had substantial accomplishments in science and technology; both had

extensive markets. Eighteenth-century China and Japan had agricultural pro-
ductivity and standards of living equal or greater than that of contemporary
European nations. . . . Government regulation and interference in the economy
was modest in Asia, for the simple reason that most economic activity took
place in free markets run by merchants and local communities, and was beyond
the reach of the limited government bureaucracies of advanced organic societies to regulate in detail. Cultural conservatism did keep economic activities
in these societies on familiar paths, but those paths allowed of considerable
incremental innovation and long-term economic growth.[6]

Well, they allowed *Smithian* "long-term economic growth"—but nothing
like the explosion of the Great Enrichment. And that's the puzzle.

There grew up in Britain during the early eighteenth century a group
of interests that had by then a stake in free markets and all the more so
eighty years later in the expanding free-trade area of the newly United
States. Article I, section 10 of the Constitution of 1789 declares that "no
state shall, without the consent of the Congress, lay any imposts or du-
ties on imports or exports." When the new rhetoric gave license for new
businesses, the businesses could enrich enough people to create their own
vested interests for opposing a mercantilist monopoly for enrichment of
a local elite. If the blue laws now enforced in the state of Indiana were re-
laxed, the grocery stores would in a while form an interest group prevent-
ing the reimposition of the law about cold-beer sales that has artificially
favored liquor stores. In the past few centuries such new interests have
bred toleration for creative destruction, and for unpredictable lives, and
for producing and earning much more than the grandparents. India did
not return to overregulation and protectionism after Manmohan Singh
had left the scene. Modi kept liberalizing, though favoring a Hindu nationalism that may yet trip India up in its rush to riches. It seems unlikely
that any future government of China will wholly reverse the commercially
tested reforms. (Xi Jinping, though, is trying.) As North, Wallis, and Weingast put it, "Creative economic destruction produces a constantly shifting distribution of economic interests, making it difficult for political of-
ficials to solidify their advantage through rent-creation."[7]

The running of markets and exchange in *towns*, and therefore what I
am calling the strictly bourgeois life—not merely its hunter-gatherer an-
ticipations in middlemen dealing in beads and boomerangs—is of course
not ancient at the scale of tens of thousands of years, because towns
came with settled agriculture during the ten thousand years before the

Common Era. What is now Oman at the eastern tip of Arabia was by 2500 BCE an urbanized middleman between the Indus Valley civilization hundreds of miles to the east in what is now Pakistan and the Sumerian civilization hundreds of miles northwest up the Persian Gulf in what is now Iraq.[8] Monica Smith notes of India in the Early Historic Period (the first few centuries BCE and CE), that despite feeble states, "archaeological and historical documentation indicates a thriving trade in a variety of goods" supported by such nonstate activities as merchant guilds forming "guild armies" to protect trade and pilgrims (compare the Hanse towns of late medieval Europe with their fleets for suppressing piracy).[9] Her town of Kaudinyapura in central India, for example, with about seven hundred souls, consumed sandstone (for grinding pestles), mica (to make the pottery shine), and rice, none of which were available locally: merchants brought them from at least fifty miles away. As Adam Smith said, "when the division of labor has been once thoroughly established . . . every man thus lives by exchanging, or becomes in some measure a merchant, and the society itself grows to be what is properly a commercial society."[10]

The point is that "commercial society" with its bourgeois specialists in commerce is by no means a late "stage" in human history. It comes with towns and is anticipated anyway by trade even without towns. And its ideology was at length remade into liberalism.

CHAPTER THIRTEEN

The Word's the Thing

What changed in Europe, and then the world, was not the material conditions of society or "commercialization" or a new security of property but the *rhetoric* of trade and production and betterment—that is, the way influential people deployed a liberal rhetoric about earning a living, such as Defoe, Voltaire, Montesquieu, Hume, Turgot, Franklin, Smith, Paine, Wilkes, Condorcet, Pitt, Sieyes, Napoleon, Godwin, Humboldt, Wollstonecraft, Bastiat, Martineau, Mill, Manzoni, Macaulay, Peel, and Emerson. And then almost everyone commenced talking this way, with the exception of an initially tiny group of antibourgeois clerisy gathering strength after 1848, such as Carlyle, List, Carey, Flaubert, Ruskin, and Marx. (Until I read the brilliant biography of him by Walls in 2017, I thought Thoreau was properly on the list of anticommercial clerisy; he was not.) The bourgeois talk was challenged mainly by appeal to traditional values, aristocratic or religious, developing into theorized nationalism, racism, socialism, eugenics, and environmentalism, and their illiberal fruit.

The change in England circa 1700, a Bourgeois Revaluation, was the coming of a business-respecting civilization accepting of the Bourgeois Deal, as Art Carden and I have put it: "You let me, a bourgeoise, make commercially tested betterments, and in the third act of the drama I will make all of *you* richer."[1] Much of the elite, and then also much of the nonelite of northwestern Europe and its offshoots, came to accept or even admire the bourgeois values of exchange and betterment. Or at least it did not attempt to block them, and even sometimes honored them on a scale never before seen. Especially the elite did so in the new United States.

Then the elites and then the common people in more of the world—and now, startlingly, in China and India—undertook to respect or at least not to bitterly despise and overtax the bourgeoisie. Not everyone did, even in the United States, and there's the rub.

The machines of materialism weren't individually necessary. There were substitutes for each of them, as Alexander Gerschenkron argued long ago.[2] They were gears in the mechanical watch, I have noted, not the spring. And some version of a jointly necessary set, such as peace and property rights, was anciently available in many, many places from Japan to England well before liberalism arose to put the gears into frenetic motion.

Surprisingly, what seem at first the most nonmaterial, nonmechanical of things—words, metaphors, narratives, ethics, ideology—were sufficient, considering the routineness of the merely necessary material conditions. There were no substitutes in the Great Enrichment for bourgeois talk. Followership after the first enrichment has been another matter, of course, and can suppress the talk, at least for a while. With techniques borrowed from bourgeois societies a Stalin could suppress bourgeois talk and yet make a lot of steel. In 1700, however, the absence of the new dignity for merchants and inventors in Britain would have led to the crushing of enterprise, as it had always been crushed before. Governments would have stopped betterment to protect the vested interests, as they always had done before—and as in an age of social democracy the governments are busy doing again, as before. Gifted people would have opted for careers as soldiers or priests or courtiers, as always, and nowadays as politicians and civil servants. The hobby of systematic (it was called "scientific") inquiry that swept Britain in the early eighteenth century would have remained in the parlor and not rapidly transitioned to the engine. The slow transition to the engine was seen in France and Italy and Germany and would have remained stuck in first gear without the stimulus of the British example, and before the British the Dutch.

The talk mattered whether or not the talk had exactly its intended effect. In the late eighteenth century a male and female public that eagerly read Hannah More and William Cowper encouraged an admiration for sober, middle-class values in hymns and novels and books of instruction. It constituted "an expanding literate public seeking not only diversion but instruction."[3] Similarly, the Abbé Sieyes' essay of 1789, *What Is the Third Estate?*, had a lasting influence on French politics. In *The Rhetoric of Bourgeois Revolution*, the historian William Sewell argues that "the literary devices that characterized Sieyes's rhetoric of social revolution quickly became standard elements in a revolutionary rhetorical lexicon. His language, it seems fair to say, had . . . enduring and powerful effects on French political culture."[4] As Tocqueville famously put it in 1856, "Our [French] men of letters did not merely impart their revolutionary ideas to the French nation; they also shaped the national temperament and outlook on life. In the long process of molding men's minds to their ideal pattern their task was all the easier since the French had had no training in the field of politics, and thus they had a clear field."[5] But in the North American British colonies from Vermont to Georgia and in the new nation made out of them—places with a good deal of local experience in the field of politics—the *rhetoric* of the American Declaration of Independence or the Gettysburg Address or the Four Freedoms speech or the I Have a Dream speech had lasting, enduring, and powerful effects in molding people's minds—or shaming them into implementing such glorious ideals. Langston Hughes sang in 1936, "O, let America be America again—/ The land that never has been yet—/ And yet must be—the land where every man is free."[6] Words supported a change in attitude toward what had always been a hardworking bourgeoisie, peasantry, and proletariat. Now all the commoners were permitted to have a go, at any rate in the American ideal.

The word's the thing, I say. Modernity did not arise from deep psychosocial changes, such as Max Weber posited in 1905. Weber's evidence was of course the talk of people: after all, talk is the natural sort of evidence for such an issue. But he believed he was getting deeper, into the core of their psychosocial being. Yet it was not a Protestant ethic or a rise of "possessive individualism" or a rise of national feeling or an "industrious revolution" or a new experimental attitude or any other change in people's deep behavior as individuals that initiated the new admiration for commercially tested betterment. These were not trivial, and were surely the flourishing branches of a new, bourgeois civilization. They were branches, however, not the root. People have always been proud and hardworking and acquisitive and curious when circumstances warranted it. From the beginning, for example, greed has been a sin and prudent self-interest a virtue. Achilles rails against Agamemnon's greed. There's nothing early modern about such sins and virtues. As for the pride of nationalism, Italian cities in the thirteenth century (or for that matter Italian parishes anywhere down to the present) evinced a local "nationalism"—the Italians still call the local version *campanilismo*, from *campanile*, the church bell tower from whose bells the neighborhood takes its daily rhythms—that would do proud a patriotic Frenchman of 1914. And as for the Scientific Revolution, it paid off late, very late. Without a new dignity for the bourgeois engineers and entrepreneurs, its tiny material payoffs in the eighteenth and early nineteenth centuries would have been disdained and the much later and then larger payoffs postponed forever.

Yet Weber was correct that cultures and societies and economies require an animating spirit, a *Geist*, an earnest rhetoric of the transcendent, and that such rhetoric matters to economic performance.[7] (Weber's word *Geist* is less incense smelling in German than its English translation of "spirit," cognate with "ghost.") The *Geist* of betterment, though, is not deep. It is superficial, located in the way people talk.

Such a rhetoric can be changed, sometimes quickly. It is not always the centuries-long "culture" that economists like to posit so that they can stop thinking about its economic effects. For example, the conservatives in the United States during the 1980s and 1990s attacked the maternal metaphor of the New Deal and the Great Society, replacing it with a paternal metaphor of discipline.[8] In China the talk (and admittedly also the police action) of the Communist Party down to 1978 stopped all good economic betterment in favor of backyard blast furnaces and gigantic collective farms. Afterward, the regime gradually allowed betterment, and by now China buzzes with talk of this or that opportunity to turn a *yuan*. So does India now, with the appropriate substitutions in currency and ultimate goals. Sometimes, as around the North Sea 1517 to 1789, the rhetoric can change even after it has been frozen for millennia in aristocratic and then also in Christian frames of antibourgeois talk. Rhetoric as cause lacks Romantic profundity. But for all that it is more encouraging, less racist, less hopeless, less nationalistic, less deterministic, less materialist.

Consider twentieth-century history in the Anglosphere. Look at how quickly under McKinley, then Teddy Roosevelt, and then Woodrow Wilson a previously isolationist United States came to carry a big stick in the world to the disgust of liberal critics such as H. L. Mencken and latterly Robert Higgs.[9] Look at how quickly the rhetoric of working-class politics changed in Britain between the elections of 1918 and 1922, crushing the great Liberal Party. Look at how quickly the rhetoric of free speech changed in the United States after 1919 through the dissenting opinions of Holmes and Brandeis.[10] Look at how legal prohibitions in Britain directed at advertisements for jobs or housing saying "Europeans only," which had been commonplace in the 1960s, changed the conversation. (As late as

1991 such rhetoric was still permitted in Germany: a pub in Frankfurt had a notice on the door, *Kein Zutritt für Hunde und Türken:* "No entry for dogs and Turks."[11]) Look at how quickly American apartheid changed under the pressure of the Freedom Riders and the Voting Rights Act (which, incidentally, my father Robert G. McCloskey helped draft in a form that withstood legal challenges). Racist talk and racist behavior, of course, didn't vanish overnight in any of these countries. But the racist talk could no longer claim the dignity of law and custom, and the behavior itself was on the run. Witness Barack Obama, or the reaction in the age of Trump. Rhetoric rules.

Look, again, at how quickly employment for married women became routine. Simone de Beauvoir, Betty Friedan, and other carriers of feminism mattered. Look at how quickly in Australia under Bob Hawke and Paul Keating in the 1980s the protectionist "Federation Settlement" dating from the early 1900s was dropped. Look at how quickly under New Labour the nationalizing Clause IV of the British Labour Party fell out of favor. Tony Blair and his rhetoric of realism mattered, despite the temporary swing back to nationalization in Jeremy Corbyn, like the swing back to racism in Trump. One can reasonably assert some material causes for parts of all these, surely. But rhetoric mattered, too, and was subject to startlingly rapid change.

The historian David Landes, as I have noted, asserted in 1998 that "if we learn anything from the history of economic development, it is that culture makes all the difference. (Here Max Weber was right on.)"[12] He was mistaken, if "culture" here means, as Landes did intend it to mean, historically deep national characteristics. We learn instead from the history of economic development that superficial *rhetoric* makes all the difference, refigured in each generation. That's a more cheerful conclusion, I have noted, than that the fault that we are underlings is in our ancient race or class or nationality or stars, not in our present speech. As the economists William Baumol, Robert Litan, and Carl Schramm put it in 2007, "There are too many examples of countries turning their economies around in a relatively short period of time, a generation or less [Korea, Singapore, Thailand, Ireland, Spain]. . . . These successes cannot be squared with the culture-is-everything view."[13] The same could be said of countries turning their politics around in a short period of time, with little change in deep culture: consider after World War II, a defeated Germany, an enriched Taiwan, at length a Franco-less Spain, then a Soviet-free Ukraine. Culture is not much to the point, it would seem—unless, indeed, "culture" is understood as the rhetoric people presently find persuasive. In which case, yes, right on.

The argument here is that contrary to a notion of essences derived from a Romantic theory of personality—and contrary also to the other side of the Romantic coin, a notion of preknown preferences derived from a utilitarian theory of decision without rhetorical reflection—what we do is to some large degree determined by how we talk to others and to ourselves. That is to say, it is a matter of public ethics, such as the twentieth century's honoring of a free press or the nineteenth century's acceptance of the Bourgeois Deal or the eighteenth century's egalitarian ethos of letting ordinary people have a go. As the French political theorist Bernard Manin put it, "The free individual is not one who already knows absolutely what he wants, but one who has incomplete preferences and is trying by means of interior deliberation and dialogue with others to determine precisely what he does want."[14] Manin points out that before the letter, in 1755, Rousseau mixed the Romantic and the utilitarian hostilities to such a democratic rhetoric into a nasty and influential concoction, which precisely denied deliberation and rhetoric.[15] Just vote, or discern without even troublesome voting the general will.

The German Reformation, the Dutch revolt, the English and American and French revolutions bred a new cheekiness among the commoners, unique for a while to northwestern Europe. The four northern European Rs were (Protestant) Reformation, (Dutch) revolt, and (English, American, and French) revolution, and (Gutenberg's) "readin'" supporting them all. In the eighteenth century there came in consequence a fifth R, a revaluation of a bourgeoisie newly prevented by a new ideology of liberalism from exercising ancient monopolies and forced therefore by the commercial test of profit to produce a universal betterment. (The Renaissance, seen usually if erroneously as a birth of individuality, is not one of the founding five Rs: it was antibourgeois, anticommoner, a celebration of the glittering lives of Federigo da Montefeltro of Urbino or Cosimo de' Medici of Florence. No wonder the formerly bourgeois northern Italians fell deeply in love with aristocracy and military uniforms and the staging of deadly and finally comical duels.) The liberty and dignity accorded commoners stimulated also the age of exploration and the Scientific Revolution and the Scottish Enlightenment, and what we are here concerned with, the greatest of these, the Great Enrichment. Not the Renaissance.

The old bourgeoisie and the aristocracy claimed to flee from the dishonor of free trade. It was sixteenth-century Dutch and English merchants, with their ink-stained hands, who developed I have noted the notion of an experimental and observing life.[16] The honor of kings and dukes and bishops was to be devalued. The devaluation of courts and politics followed, slowly. What followed centuries later in India and elsewhere was acceptance of the Bourgeois Deal and the commercially tested betterment and supply characteristic of an enriching modern world. Long may it triumph for the good of the wretched of the earth.

PART III
The Doubts

CHAPTER FOURTEEN

Doubts by Analytic Philosophers about the Killer App Are Not Persuasive

A mong various commentators on my answer to the leading question in modern economic and historical science—Why are we so rich now?—are two philosophers, a sociologist, a political theorist, and an economic historian who commented all at once on *Bourgeois Equality*, the third volume of the trilogy that set out the killer app of humanomics. Theirs was a stiff challenge to humanomics and its application to explaining modern economic growth.[1]

The philosopher Gerald Gaus's overgenerous praise startled me—I didn't set out to write a "great work" and am reluctant to think it is anything close (I blush).[2] I merely intended in the trilogy, and in particular the third volume on which Gaus focuses, to redeem the bourgeoisie and to find out the scientific truth about its role, and especially the role of attitudes toward it, in making the modern world. Around the year 2000 I thought the job would take one volume. In the end in 2016 it took some 1,700 pages, through-composed (that is, little was published as articles before each book was finished).

The main reason I stopped at three volumes—the third volume being even longer than the other two very stout ones—was articulated by the philosopher of religion Alvin Plantinga justifying stopping at his own third volume on warranted belief: "A trilogy is perhaps unduly self-indulgent, but a tetralogy [not to speak of the hexology I once contemplated] is unforgivable."[3] Or to use the theological term from translations of the Hebrew for sins suitable for stoning to death, an abomination.

You don't write some 1,700 pages of evidence and reasoning about history and economics and ethics and the rest as though writing a bank draft (to quote the young Kant's protest against the methodical habits that he later was taught by his dear, dear friend Mr. Green), with a preplanned and routine outcome. The experience is less like central planning and more like the discovery in commercially tested betterment. Over the twenty years of thinking and reading, within which were the twelve years of publishing, I hope I made a few discoveries. The chief methodological discovery, of which I am trying to persuade you in the present book, is that economics and history need humanomics. The chief substantive discovery is the one I outlined in the four previous chapters: that the one essential and sufficient cause of the modern world—the central pole of the tent, in the old figure of speech, or the spring in the mechanical watch in a somewhat less old one—is a cause much more potent than, say, any Weberian psychological change in the direction of better bourgeois behavior or Northian change of Samuelsonian incentives or Marxian inevitability of historical materialism. The spring was the sociological and political change unique to northwestern Europe for the first time accepting the bourgeoisie and its fruits. It was the ideology of liberalism. The change in ideology made ordinary people bold, leading to a parallel ideology of an "innovism" (what is lamentably called "capitalism"). It permitted and encouraged masses if ordinary people to have a go. It was, in Smith's phrase, "the liberal plan of equality, liberty, and justice."[4] It permitted people to be inventive and therefore rich and, if they wished, cultivated. Thus *Bourgeois Equality*.

Yet Gerald Gaus, listening intently to one John W. Chapman's theories, says that I didn't "get it *entirely* right."[5] His theme is that I am insufficiently game-theoretic and institutional and therefore miss my own best point. He asserts, against what he thinks is my (1905 Weberian, psychological, *Die protestantische Ethik und der Geist des Kapitalismus*) point, that "there is strong reason to question the explanatory power of character traits and attitudes."[6]

Yet on the contrary, I am saying that it was *not* the Weberian character traits of the bourgeois, but the *ideology* of those around them, that changed. Or if you want an older word that Marx did not invent, it's the social *rhetoric* that changed. Or if you want a less contentious word, also ancient, the social *ethics* changed.

The misunderstanding is surprising coming from Gaus. He is usually a better reader. He must have started from some strong prior conviction, which made it hard for him to discern the present point. What prior? He appears to thank that my main opponent is the late lamented Douglass North and his neoinstitutional followers. I admit to arguing against North a little in the present volume and a lot in the other of the pair now, and for at least part of the *Bourgeois Dignity* that Gaus is commenting on, and in a few other essays.[7] But Gaus thinks that my opposition to North is self-deceived, probably on my part merely envious and cantankerous, not a substantive scientific difference. He thinks I am fooling myself by opposing North. He wants me to recover North's focus on "the institutional rules of the game" by way of the philosopher Christina Bicchieri's game-theoretic logic, "the rule-governance of social morality."[8] He's slouching towards North. And anyway he's slouching towards an economistic line of argument that notably neglects the autonomous role of ideas. That is to say, Gaus doubts humanomics without realizing that it is what I am peddling. And humanomics, you know, is the *main* point of the present book. The scientific history of the Great Enrichment in *Bourgeois Dignity* exhibits, I realized later, that very humanomics.

Economism of course has some merit—I do not want my union card as an economist, Harvard Local 02136 and Chicago Local 60637, to be taken away. But game theory is something like the opposite of what I came to argue in the trilogy and now argue here. Another way to understand the three volumes (and the present volume, seen as drawing the implication for economics more broadly) is the working out in ethics and history and sociology and literature of an escape from the Prudence-Only character that lies at the heart of Samuelsonian economics. Despite North's protestations, he and his followers espouse a highly conventional Prudence-Only, materialist, Max U, a "neoclassical," noncooperative game-theory notion of people and societies. I wish they wouldn't. I wish they would grow up and notice that people think and love and argue. It's the force of language, I have argued above, expressing human action, not merely re-action. As Smith said, "everyone is practicing oratory on others thro the whole of his life."[9]

Gaus declares that "modern ethics concerns what we *must* do—what we are required to do even if we are not attracted to it."[10] Shades of Kant and deontology. I do wish that philosophers would extract themselves from their attachment to the Sage of Köningsberg. He admitted no rhetoric, no oratory, no ideology, no anthropology: we are scientists of society, he implied, and don't deal with such stuff. Gaus wants there to be rigid rules, and he wants them to have a no-talk, game-theoretic support. Thus

North again, and Avner Greif.[11] "Does [a good person] ascribe to bourgeois virtue? [Note again that he thinks it is the individual, psychological
behavior of the bourgeoisie I am talking about instead of the sociology
and politics of how others value it.] I don't know. Must she act in the required way? Certainly."[12] This is Kant indeed, the attempt to build ethics on what every *rational* actor *must* ascribe to, never mind what actual
French people actually do. *Sie müssen.*

In the words of an old *New Yorker* cartoon quoting a toddler kicking
in a high chair against a dinner he doesn't like, "I say it's spinach, and I say
to hell with it."

Though I admire his philosophical history of the egalitarianism of
hunter-gathering and rely on it in *Bourgeois Equality*, Gaus is not a particularly historical thinker. That's all right. One can't do everything. It's
good to hear for example about his experiment, coauthored with Shaun
Nichols, showing that "a social morality that stresses [minimally just] prohibitions rather than [prearranged, hierarchically granted] permissions
encourages innovation and exploratory action."[13] It's an interesting result
that fits with my argument that liberalism above all made the modern
world. As I said in *Bourgeois Equality*, the same observation about behavior is typical of Hume and Smith and Kant and one side of *Aufklärung*. It
is liberal ideology in contrast with Colbert's mercantilism.

I do wish Gaus would realize, though, that we need to solve a *historical* as much as an economic problem, namely, why the Great Enrichment
happened when and where it did, in a bit of northwestern Europe beginning in the past two or three centuries and then spreading to the world.
The purely economic arguments, as I showed at some length, especially
in the second volume, *Bourgeois Dignity*, have this problem: that China,
for example, had coal and India a massive foreign trade and Spain a great
overseas empire and the Ottomans the rule of law and France an Enlightenment, yet none initiated the Great Enrichment.

That's the trouble with timeless arguments from game theory, such as
Bicchieri's or North's or Acemoglu's. In one sense they explain too much
because their mechanisms are universal. In another sense they explain too
little because they do not attend to the ideational peculiarity of the Dutch
and English bits of northwestern Europe—namely, the peculiarity of a
nascent liberalism. Gaus notes that "in the last fifteen years a large body
of evidence has accumulated that the actions of humans are critically sensitive to the normative expectations of others."[14] I might remark that we
hardly need evidence from "the last fifteen years" for such an ancient and

obvious feature of human nature (*Antigone*? The Hebrew Prophets? *The Mahabharata*?), but I entirely agree. And it is a quite *different* notion than the Better Bourgeois that Gaus thinks I am claiming. "The critical point is that ['trendsetters,' in Bicchieri's vocabulary] were able to shape the social rules that generated normative expectations supporting equal dignity, liberty, markets and innovation, and that these normative expectations were widely accepted as legitimate."[15] Sure.

All right, but then why then and there? That's the historico-scientific puzzle. The Bicchierian logic would apply to the Roman Republic or to early modern Japan, which didn't produce the modern world. My books try to explain *why* then and there, first in Holland and then in Britain, and find that it was a close thing, but decidedly ideological, a matter of ideas. The ideas of course themselves had causes, some of them material (European "discovery" of the New World, European orientation toward the sea, European political fragmentation) but many of them ideational (the Radical Reformation's attack on church hierarchy, Joel Mokyr's community of scientists, the rights of man, and woman). Gaus declares that "A framework of liberal equality embraces this ideal of universal membership in the community: the rules of basic social life apply equally to all, simply as members of a community."[16] But that's the liberal ideology on which I put more and more emphasis in the trilogy as I wrote it, culminating in the political book in 2019 from Yale University Press, *Why Liberalism Works*.

"The moral rules of the game," writes Gaus, channeling North again, obtain "when we confront total strangers. In most cases we know little about these strangers—in particular, their conception of virtue and how well they live up to what they consider virtuous—yet we need to rely on them. How can that happen?"[17]

It happened anciently. It is not true that there was an internal, psychological "development" of honesty, for example. There was on the contrary in northwestern Europe a new public *honoring* of commercial honesty, which is an entirely different matter, a matter of ideology or rhetoric or ethics, taking place historically and sociologically, not economically and psychologically. The evidence is strong, as for example in shifts of meaning from aristocratic to bourgeois in the very word *honest*.[18]

Aside from these textual matters, I must say I find myself repelled by Gaus's vision of people as cynical conformists: "we are such deeply social normative creatures, in the sense that we are so attuned to the normative expectations of others, that we can achieve a stable rule-based system of cooperation even when many are not enthusiastic about the moral attitudes and virtues that the rules express." I invite him to reread Thucydides's dialogue between the Athenian diplomats and the Melians, and repent.[19] "A critical explanatory variable for many people," Gaus writes, "is their responsiveness to the normative expectations of those with whom they share a social life."[20] I agree, and said so repeatedly, though not on the basis of game theory construed as a complete social science (as my friendly acquaintances Gintis and Bowles, admired by Gaus, do try to construe it; I recommend for a more sensible version Field 2003).[21] "I believe," he writes, "that it is, in general, false that everyday moral action requires virtues such as temperance or courage, or even the 'middling' virtues, except in so far as one must be sensitive to the legitimate expectations of others."[22] This other-directed, contemporaneous (as against, say, the developmental story of Confucius or Adam Smith), Nash-equilibrium concept of "virtue" is a strange characterization of most of the beautiful minds I know, including that of Gerald Gaus. The courageous pursuit of truth that characterizes his work, for example, would be reduced in his theory to conformist careerism. "We should never underestimate just how important conformity is to any culture."[23] So Gaus evidently believes, at any rate when he is thinking theoretically. "Most, I think, seem essentially driven by what they expect others will do, and what they believe are the legitimate normative expectations of others."[24] This, I have to say, is nuts. Or spinach.

On the other hand, I admit that the economist in me delights in Gaus/North/Bicchieri/Acemoglu/Gintis games. And I *like* spinach.

*   *   *

The philosopher Jennifer Baker gets it. I've dabbled in philosophy, most explicitly in 1994 in *Knowledge and Persuasion in Economics*. But I know very well that I am an amateur compared with the present-day genuine philosophers I've known moderately well through their works and their persons, such as Bill Hart, John Nelson, Steve Fuller, Eric Schliesser, Loren Lomasky, Uskali Mäki, Jack Vromen, Richard Rorty, Martha Nussbaum, David Schmidtz, Sam Fleischacker, Alfred Saucedo, and Atanacio Hernandez. What regularly astonishes me about philosophers, whether analytic or Continental, on ethics or on epistemology, is their ability to make distinctions, often important ones. *Analysis* means in Greek "cut apart." Baker neatly cuts apart, for example, my argument into nine "implausible assumptions the [hypothesis of the Bourgeois] Deal avoids."[25]

Baker's own project here is to ask "how to think about the 'haves' when you are a 'have not,'" which, she says (pretty much correctly) "is missing in McCloskey's approach."[26] "Non-bourgeois values amount to a rather intact philosophical outlook."[27] Agreed, they do, and keep surfacing (as in Donald Trump's views on foreign trade), which is one reason I wrote the trilogy—to contradict them.

"I do not know how McCloskey would write for this audience" of have-nots.[28] I admit that I'm writing mainly to the clerisy, saying to it, Get over your hatred of the bourgeoisie. I say to the bourgeoisie itself, Stop apologizing but start getting serious about your own ethical commitments. But I could write to the poor, too, and, as she suggests I should. After all, I got into economics and stayed in it to help the poor and to honor all our impoverished ancestors, among them mine. "The unequal distribution of the goods of this world is considered to be efficacious for reasons mere humans cannot access is a very particular viewpoint, particularly support-ive of commercially tested betterment."[29] Yes, it is a view particular to a modern view of economics, Schumpeterian, even. You see it even in Rawls. It doesn't much appeal to actual poor people, only to their soi-disant defenders from the left or from liberalism.

But that is why we need, in getting the poor onto the program, an *ideology* supporting what Hayek dubbed the Great Society. Demonstration effects, such as the utter ruin of the Venezuelan economy recently or the startling enrichment since 1978 of coastal China or the American Dream fulfilled even now by most Americans, do support a faithful bourgeois ideology. But St. Paul observed that "faith is assurance of things hoped for, a conviction of things *not* seen" (Heb. 11.1). Keep the faith. It's hard. After every major financial crash, the worst being after 1929, but again a pretty bad one after 2008, and the COVID-19 wreckage in 2020, the fragile faith erodes the Bourgeois Deal—what she calls the "very par-ticular viewpoint." It is challenged from the working class itself in votes for populists. And it has always been challenged since 1848 from the left clerisy helpfully telling the working class what to think about the terrible problems of markets, bankers, alienation, inequality, and the lack of jobs for the clerisy to correct the horribly imperfect economy—which deliv-ered meanwhile to the working class a 3,000 percent increase in real in-come per person.

Baker thinks there is a problem of the have-nots perceiving the dem-onstrations of the "particular viewpoint." "If the horrors of present-day Venezuela are used to convince low wage workers that the [Bourgeois]

Deal we have is fair, it is still the case that low wage workers have less to lose in such a transition."[30] I see her point. So did Count Bismarck, who declared in a speech in 1889, as he persuaded the Reichstag to pass an old-age pension, "I will consider it a great advantage when we have 700,000 small pensioners [then nearly the entire population of men over age sixty in the German Empire] drawing their annuities from the state, especially if they belong to those classes who otherwise do not have much to lose by an upheaval."[31] Poor people regularly think *La Revolución* will make them better off. What the hell, Archie, what the hell. Usually it only makes the poor "better off" relatively, by equalizing misery. Hang the bankers from the lampposts, invade the houses of the rich. And end up as poor as Cuba, in which real income per person has not risen since 1959. (Yet Baker is right that a few of the have-nots, and most of the left clerisy, still think that Cuba is a workers' paradise. I wish they would visit and watch and listen.)

My claim, and in the end I think Baker's, too, is that philosophy in such matters should be, as Dick Rorty used to say, edifying, persuading people to the good life, and *not* accepting their sin of envy as an acceptable preference by Max U. "I do not see that McCloskey has yet confronted a non-elite, non-bourgeois ethos as if it had normative content at odds with the terms of the original [Bourgeois] Deal."[32] True. But our task is edification, that is, changing the minds of the poor (and of the clerisy and the bourgeoisie). I want the poor to become bourgeois in spirit and to admire the bourgeoisie. There are bad versions, like a peasant admiring the Glorious King, the poor American worker in Toledo, entranced by neofascism, admiring the Rich Donald. It's not a liberal ideology. But it is certainly an ideology, and it speaks to the poor.

Yet American workers are commonly *not* envious, which distinguishes the American from the European or Asian or African poor. Americans, it has often been noted, are unusually bourgeois, and even poor Americans are so. "Are non-elite, non-clerisy, low wage workers satisfied with what they have already received in the aftermath of the Bourgeois Deal?"[33] No, of course they aren't. No one is ever satisfied. I should get more. You, too. Not so sure about those others. But the edifying task is to persuade them to an ideology that enriches the world, not to inflame them with envy or anger, as Progressivism or Trumpism does.

"This is the boldest of my claims," Baker writes, "a fourth modification to create a viable Deal with low wage workers: engage with them philosophically. Not over personal values or way of life, but over the issues of our mutual welfare and what we owe others."[34] Yes: edification. "Of course an ethicist like me would see a role for ethical explanation."[35] Yes. I take the ethical justification, expressed most fully in *The Bourgeois Virtues: Ethics for An Age of Commerce*, to be justifying the ways of God to man, or more exactly justifying the ways of the Great Society to its people.

"I wonder," she continues, "would McCloskey both convince the working class of this [Great Society of commercially tested betterment] and make them care about it?"[36] I earnestly hope so. Taking on the Baker critique, I promise in future to think more about reaching the working class. I do not think the left clerisy reaches it, actually. The clerisy imagines solidarity, but only on the hard left's top-down terms or else on the soft left's let's-sing-kumbaya terms. Consider Leninism and the leading role of the Party, staffed of course from the clerisy.

I have already, though, one simple thought about reaching the working class. It is something I learned long ago from a political theorist at the University of Iowa, John Nelson, namely, that the popular artists making movies and rock music are the formers of ideology. Professors of philosophy and economics and sociology and political science are swell. But the below-highbrow art is where the rubber meets the road, as we say in country music.

"What would it take," Baker asks, "for McCloskey to agree with the 'clerisy' that low wage workers have suffered grave losses of dignity in our current-day society?"[37] It would take a history that did not in fact happen, the fairy-scary tale by Howard Zinn or Charles Sellers (from the left, suggestively parallel with Trump's scaremongering from the right), because low-wage workers were once *utterly* disdained. Look at Blacks. And almost all your ancestors.

Similarly, Baker asks in a footnote, "is a 'peasant's view' of markets a realistic one (for the time) or not?"[38] In a zero-sum society like the one Jesus of Nazareth faced, it is realistic, but only roughly, since even with no big growth there is a modest gain to be had from trade, as Jesus the carpenter surely knew. But to get the big positive sum of the Great Enrichment, a factor of thirty or one hundred, we have to have an ideology supporting commercially tested betterment. The ideology does not necessarily have to be in every detail correct, but it has to be an ideology nonetheless. As I said at one point,

Marxians call the acceptance of such betterment "false consciousness," a con job. Ideologies are indeed con jobs, whether good cons or bad. In psychiatry, false consciousness is called "lack of insight." If you as the patient don't agree with the psychiatrist's ideology you are said to exhibit such a lack. But unless the masses in a democracy accept betterment they can be led by populists or Bolsheviks or fascists to rise up and kill the goose. That's another con job, with worse consequences. Killing the golden goose has never been good for the poor.[39]

CHAPTER FIFTEEN

Nor by Sociologists or Political Philosophers

I can't possibly claim the great sociologist Jack Goldstone misunderstands the book. His lucid and elegant summary deserves some sort of prize for scholarly temperance. Goldstone summarizes my argument thus:

> What can prevent the elite from preventing change, when the status quo so strongly favors their interests? An insistence that ordinary people should be encouraged to act independently, be respected for originality and innovation, and be allowed to retain (most of) the profits of any activities they offer in free and fair markets.[1]

Spot on.

Yet Goldstone doubts, with Gaus, that I have got it *entirely* right. "Why did the shift in rhetoric to value the bourgeoisie *in England* not simply evolve as it did in all other cases, namely to create an oligarchy of privileged merchants who still derided ordinary citizens?"[2] It's an important question, to which I offered in the book in various places only a sketch of an answer, referring for example to the accidents following the struggle between Stuarts and Parliament, 1625 to 1688, with a thoroughly bourgeois example of the Dutch Republic at hand. Had Charles I and especially James II not been both so similar to Charles's father and James's grandfather—the James VI of Scotland who became also James I of England, "the wisest fool in Christendom"—it might have turned out differently.

The other doubt is more fundamental. Goldstone asks, "How does anyone acquire the belief—based on no prior successful examples in history—that the best way to innovate is to perform thousands of experiments to create new products or processes as Wedgewood did to create Jasper blue (as McCloskey points out on p. 522)?"[3] He argues, therefore, that "it could not just have been respect that produced their extraordinarily productive innovations. Something else must have happened as well," in particular the new engineering culture that Goldstone and Joel Mokyr and Margaret Jacob have emphasized as special to the Europe of the Scientific Revolution and the Industrial Enlightenment.[4] The point persuades, though one wonders at the implicit claim that an obsession with experiment did not also characterize many people in other cultures (Mayan? Chinese? Byzantine?) whose scientific culture we happen now to know so much less about. And doesn't widespread admiration for an activity—whether wielding a sword or celebrating the mass or performing an experiment—inflame the ambition of the young?

But wait. Goldstone's first doubt concerning my argument was that the elite would usually stop progress yet didn't in Britain. But the Bourgeois Revaluation that the book touts did in fact reverse such an ideology of protection, replacing it with an ideology of liberalism, the "innovism" that I would like people to use instead of the idiotic and misleading "capitalism." We need to look into how and why it happened. And it is what the book does. To the correct observation that Britain is just where the elite did *not* stop progress, the book notes (pp. 629–30, but in numerous other places as well) that an engineering culture has to have a *mass* of innovators, a few of whom rise to the eminence of Newcomen, Smeaton, and Cartwright. Mass innovation requires exactly liberalism as a primary cause, allowing ordinary people to have a go. *Si non, non.* Or more to the point, if not, then not a vibrant Anglosphere but instead a stagnant Italy or France or even (by the eighteenth century) Holland, all of which had had vibrant scientific and engineering cultures.

"Why not a host of linked changes, to ideas, institutions, and capital," asks Goldstone, "that created a virtuous circle of cross-fertilization without a single primary cause?"[5] I often get the question why I focus on "a single primary cause," to which I reply that in science we are seeking such causes. If one or two or three pretty much suffices, we are sworn to say so. Coulomb's Law implies that the repulsions between positively charged but not massive spheres close to each other are very much stronger than . their gravitational attraction. One, therefore, can ignore the very small offsetting gravitational attraction in calculating the acceleration of the spheres away from each other. I showed in 2010 in *Bourgeois Dignity* that the other and materialist explanations of the Great Enrichment, such as institutions and capital, don't work quantitatively—not even approximately. They were dependent on liberalism or were not in fact necessary or had little economic oomph or occurred in various other parts of Eurasia also with suitable "horizontal conditions" (as Nancy Cartwright and Jeremy Hardie put it in their fine application of Cartwright's philosophy of causation).[6] So we are left with one cause, peculiar to northwestern Europe and especially, by accidents fortunate for us Anglophones, British liberalism.

Goldstone quarrels with my quarrel with neoinstitutionalists such as North and Acemoglu, or in some of their moods with Goldstone and Mokyr. He wrote in an earlier version of his comment, "Institutions are simply ideas of proper behavior that have been codified by law or custom to become normative behavior. If ideas for what is proper normative behavior undergo a major alteration, then institutions should change as well." The remark (that it didn't get into the final version show's Goldstone's reliable scientific taste) well illustrates one of my objections to neoinstitutionalism; namely, that it depends on a tautology. Let us define *institutions*, Goldstone avers, as anything that comes out of human minds. Then we can drop changes of minds tout court as causal, since *all* changes in ideas must be codified as normative in what we are calling "institutions." So much for the idea of liberalism as causal. QED.

The tautology enables a good deal of hand-waving assertions of causality in neoinstitutional circles. In Goldstone's case, for example, he vaunts "the founding of the American colonies, and major victories over Spain and France [not final, actually, until June 18, 1815] that shifted the balance of power in Europe and established Britain as a major power" as evidence that "it is hard to argue that Britain thus had no significant or rapid institutional changes prior to the 'Great Enrichment.'"[7] Well. It needs to be explained why the theme of "power and plenty," such as Ronald Findlay and Kevin H. O'Rourke put forward in an ill-considered book and which power-politics theorists thrill to monthly in the pages of *Foreign Affairs*, is anything but a category mistake.[8] Being powerful does not make you rich unless violence against others is enriching. It's hasn't been much enriching in the dramatically positive-sum world since 1800, and in truth was not much even in the old zero-sum world. Conquest is not a good business plan. Ask the Spaniards in the seventeenth century or the Russians now.

Another case of the magic of tautology is the assertion by numerous economic historians that the Dutch-inspired national debt—which allowed King Billy and Queen Anne, and then the Hanoverians, to wage almost incessant war against Spain and France until that June day at Waterloo—made for a capital market. It has never been explained why the issuing of bonds to finance the throwing away of resources in pointless warfare did anything but crowd out civilian investment. There is no question that late in the eighteenth century it did so for canal building. The neoinstitutionalist line of argument is, first, call warfare or the national debt an "institution," then apply the tautological lemma, and conclude triumphantly that institutions "matter" without having to get into the irritating weeds of economic logic or statistical measurement, not to speak of the effect of ideas on history.

But Goldstone is better than this. I have always admired his precision in the use of historical examples, as in his riff here on the Scientific Revolution. He shares with Joel Mokyr, for instance, the conviction that "by the time of Francis Bacon, it was possible to conceive of a future in which mankind had amassed more and more valuable and powerful information than ever before."[9] Surely he and Mokyr are right, although (to repeat) it needs to be acknowledged that we do not at present know enough about science and intellectual life in other places to be entirely sure that the coming of a scientific tradition was unique to Europe. The experience over the past few decades of having, after Joseph Needham, to revise radically the history of Chinese science and technology should make us a little cautious about accepting European superiority as a fact without enough actual knowledge about the non-Europeans. And anyway, if we suppose that "it was possible to conceive" of progress, are we not then dealing with an ideological change, not an institutional one (at any rate in a nontautological sense)? I think Goldstone and Mokyr would agree. The extant institutions, after all, such as the church or the monarchies or the older universities, fought the idea of progress to the death. Their death.

A big, big evidential problem with the emphasis by Goldstone, Mokyr, and Jacob on the Scientific Revolution and the Enlightenment, further, is that these were Europe-wide movements, not special to Britain. Galileo and Catherine the Great, after all, were decidedly not British. Yet the Great Enrichment down to 1851 certainly overwhelming was. Innovations in music that put it far in advance of its European forms elsewhere occurred in Italy and the German lands but exactly not in the Dutch and British heartlands of the Great Enrichment. Meanwhile the remnants of Charlemagne's empire, though by then surely enlightened, came very late to enrichment.

Before 1851, Goldstone notes, "the gains in science had the impact of inspiring a desire for innovation and providing methods for its realization, but not yet of offering discoveries that would transform economies."[10] I quite agree. Against Mokyr, I would date the economically weighty triumphs of high science to the twentieth century. Before that, inspiration to young men and some women, yes; economically large impact, no. And even the inspiration and later the impact depended on a massive extension of having a go, itself dependent on liberalism, or at any rate (to speak of chairs in chemistry in German universities) an egalitarian policy imposed by tyrants, itself inspired, as Goldstone says in his peroration, by ideas.

I emphasize liberalism, which has been set aside by most students of the matter since the 1890s, when historical materialism first captured the mind of Europe. In the end I think Goldstone would agree.

* * *

The political philosopher Sonja Amadae's point is exactly mine (and so I will register only our disagreements), namely, to resist what she calls neoliberalism, namely, the game theory that Gaus, for example, favors, and to revive the classical liberalism of Smith and Mill that "encompassed ethical commitment," as she puts it. The point on Mill has become conventional, that his ethics undergirds even his economics.[11] "The neoliberal institutionalists," such as Gaus and sometimes Mokyr, she writes, "concentrate on incentives to the exclusion of ethical reasons for action."[12]

She is of the left. I was once, too. Now I sit above the statism of both left and right, in a modern bleeding-heart version of true liberalism that rejects pushing people around for leftish or rightist programs. Such a liberalism is the "dialectic" she helpfully attributes to me. Amadae in effect wants me to declare whether or not I admire Nordic social democracy. I do, at any rate for Nordics and Minnesotans. I've lived in it. I'm not so sure it can be implemented in Italy or Illinois without crippling corruption. No reasonable Italian or Illinoisan wants to give her rulers more money and power in order to go on pretending to do lovely things for poor people while Swiss bank accounts and Wisconsin hunting lodges wax fat.

"I ask McCloskey to take a position on whether ideals can be accompanied with a commitment to a minimal safety net, to ensure the inclusion of the least well-off in the opportunities for development."[13] Glad you asked. The answer is yes. I am, as I said often in the book, a Christian libertarian, or a bleeding-heart classical liberal, or a sisterly enthusiast for free and dignified commoners. If you want the backing for such a position, see *Why Liberalism Works.*

Or if you wish, and Amadae does, I am a "dialectical libertarian." I argue in various books and articles in detail, however, that by far the best safety net is vigorous economic growth, which enriches laborers in a dignified way by much more than any coerced transfer or trade union can. And in any case an enrichment, such as in the notably "capitalist" and innovative Swedish economy after the liberalization of the 1850s, makes possible the taxes to pay for a welfare state. That is, it does unless Italian or Illinoisan politicians get to the money first.

It is clear that I need to read Amadae, and I undertake to do so. But I detect in her a (justifiable) annoyance that I haven't done so yet. On the other hand, it is pretty clear she hasn't looked into the other books in the trilogy, since many of her points are anticipated or answered by them. When Amadae notes in support of the proposition she and I share, that "non-consequentialist forms of action, including rule-following, commitment and promising, loyalty and trust, depend on reasons for action independent from satisfying preferences," she cites Sen, Hausman, and Heath, but not McCloskey (1994b), or in briefer form McCloskey (1994a), which were devoted to exactly that proposition through a virtue-ethical approach more philosophically nuanced than Sen's "commitment."[14] She says that I was "not engaging in the intricacies of the contemporary debates on this topic," which she would have known to be mistaken if she had read *The Bourgeois Virtues*—unless indeed, as I suspect is the case in her mind, the "intricacies" are to be confined to a narrow group of economic methodologists devoted to certain routine games in analytic philosophy.[15] (Had she in fact read *Knowledge and Persuasion in Economics* [1994b] she would know my detailed conclusion about the value of such routine games.) In a puzzling sentence she complains about my alleged "literary dismissal of surgically honing in on the key points of contemporary debate in favor of recounting the history of capitalism."[16] It seems to irritate her that I use evidence from literature and from history, as though routine analytic philosophy is the only way to get at "the key points." I do not think it is. There are many routes to edification. But I imagine she doesn't approve of Richard Rorty, either.

Further, she makes the same Weberian mistake that Gaus makes in attributing to me the view that the bourgeoisie just got better, exhibiting "the correct virtues of temperance and prudence."[17] No. The bourgeoisie was always thus. It is what one means by a successful merchant in, say, ancient Rome or in present-day New Delhi. What did change was (what she in the same sentence mixes up with the Weberian notion) the society's "commitment to human dignity and liberty." In a word, liberalism.

Maybe it would have been good to suggest to the reviewers here that they read, or at any rate buy, *Bourgeois Dignity*, which gives most of the economics, and also *The Bourgeois Virtues*, which gives most of the ethical philosophy. But I concede that seven hundred pages is quite a lot, and 1,700 verges on being unforgivable. (Amadae complains that I do not cite Habermas. She must have missed pages 395 and 535, not to speak of *The Bourgeois Virtues*, and my writings in the 1980s and 1990s on rhetoric, all making great use of the honored Jürgen, the German sociologist/philosopher who is usually unread because he is unreadable.) But that's many more pages than one can reasonably expect a reviewer to read. Still, even a bit of it would have saved her from making vexed if foolish remarks about what she imagines my arguments to be.

Again, in a phrase from an earlier draft that she apparently thought better of, Amadae doesn't think I present "a rigorously presented case," which suggests that she has no knowledge of *Bourgeois Dignity: Why Economics Can't Explain the Modern World*—though it could also be, I repeat, that by "rigorously presented" she again means routine analytic philosophy, not a serious engagement with all the edifying arguments and evidence.[18] She wishes "McCloskey had either acknowledged that capitalism is only statistically better on average, and that some people pay the price for economic growth."[19] Such talk is that of a political theorist who is not actually open to "only" quantitative or economic thinking. "Only statistically better on average" means, as I rigorously show throughout, upwards of a 10,000 percent increase per capita, 1800 to the present, which is of such a magnitude as to make it nearly impossible to find "some people" who "pay the price of economic growth."[20] At 100 percent, sure. At 3,000 percent, unlikely. At 10,000 percent . . . well, you see what I mean.

Therefore, *of course* the Great Enrichment has been "inclusive."[21] Only someone who disdains an engineer's sense of magnitude would think otherwise. The entire income distribution leapt out so dramatically to the right that it is virtually impossible to find someone in, say, Finland who is shorter in height or in years of life than her ancestors taken as a group, or more subject to starvation than Finns in 1866–1868, or less literate than Finns before the Compulsory School Attendance Act of 1921. And to think economically, the traditional farmers, say, whose land is bought out by developers, share in the enrichment. And the loss to harness makers that comes from the invention of the automobile is massively offset by the gain to others, and even to the harness makers now riding about in their Ford cars. "Merely" quantitative growth made virtually all Finns, whether farmers or harness makers, massively healthier, less subject to famine, and 99.98 percent literate.

But I suspect that Amadae will not be easily moved from her apparent acceptance of the conventions of leftish history. She demands that I reply to Marxist history and economics. Yet giving a reply to Marxism in some detail was in fact one of the main themes of the trilogy, or for that matter of my scholarly life from 1968 onward.[22] As was pointed out as early as Hayek (1954), the left is convinced that there must have been some original sin to explain "capitalism" (the fact of which, by the way, the British did not "invent"). So does Amadae. Such a history is defective, as the trilogy shows. One can't reply to historical claims that are defective from top to bottom, though I do keep trying.

In the Marxist, or at any rate Marxoid, fashion, for example, she criticizes me harshly for allegedly ignoring the slave trade, which criticism suggests again that she is not familiar with the other books in the trilogy. She is confident that "the gross injustices experienced by enslaved African-Americans . . . [were] arguably a crucial practice related to the hockey blade's meteoric ascent (Sherwood 2007; Baptist 2014)."[23] I know that many people such as Sherwood and Baptist argue that slavery was crucial. I also know that it makes people feel virtuous to rail against gross injustice, as slavery certainly was (or at any rate so we came to think it was after many bourgeois such as John Newton ["Amazing Grace"] and William Wilberforce instructed us). But the belief that slavery was a crucial cause of the Great Enrichment, despite the noble embodiment of such a belief in Lincoln's Second Inaugural, say, is implausible as economics or as history. There are twenty good arguments of fact against such a view. If Amadae had read outside her political comfort zone on the history of slavery she would know it.[24] For one thing, slavery was ancient, but modern economic growth was, well, modern. For another, slavery was not necessary for Western growth, as you can see for example in the acceleration of growth after slavery was abolished. For still another, output of cotton from the American South was by 1870 as high as it was under slavery in 1860. And as I just noted, it was a bourgeois "capitalist" society, especially in Britain and in the Northern United States, that worked to abolish "legalized slavery [under which] some individuals profit while others shoulder the burden."[25] We have here a common figure of argument, whether of left or right: so to speak, "I hold passionately a political conviction X; someone said something that seems to agree with X; therefore I need seek no further, for we are of the Party: X is obviously correct, and anyone who says not-X must be my enemy. McCloskey is my enemy." It's hard to learn from an enemy.

Again, she criticizes me for not dealing with inequality. The criticism is still another fashionable and un–self-critical leftism on her part. In fact I deal with inequality massively in the very book under discussion and in more pointed form in a long review of Piketty's book, revised in *Why Liberalism Works*.[26]

Amadae leaves off leftish clichés, though, and really gets going at the very end, in pages I much admire, beginning "While McCloskey's argument may be incomplete for not fully defining or explaining 'liberty,' or human dignity" (neither of her assertions here is correct, by the way, but let us go on).[27] She correctly notes that Smith had two microprinciples, one being Prudence and the other the Impartial Spectator (not the "impartial judge," as Amadae remembers the phrase; it's prudent to check such phrases in scientific disputations), both having macroconsequences.[28] I said this, at some length, calling it "Smith's other invisible hand, the social one as against the economic. We become polite members of our society by interacting on the social stage—note the word, 'inter-acting.' "[29] Amadae views me therefore as proposing "a dialectical structure that places both ethics and tangible self-betterment on a complementary footing," which suggestion I gratefully accept.[30]

CHAPTER SIXTEEN

Nor Even by Economic Historians

And finally to my beloved *vriendje*, Joel Mokyr. As you might not infer from his sometimes prickly comments, Mokyr and I agree on an immense amount, substantively and methodologically (if not in every detail politically), in economics and in history and in economic history. I started focusing on the central question of social science—as I've noted, why are we so much richer than our ancestors?—a decade after he did. He has taught me massively. Without his books I could not have written mine.

And he and I and a very few others stand together against idea-less accounts, from Marx to Freakonomics. As Mokyr writes, "Professor Mc-Closkey (p. 511) cites me as having written that 'economic change depends, more than most economists think, on what people believe.' That message [the opening sentence of his 2010 book], obvious as it may sound, needs to be stated and re-stated, to rid ourselves of the relics of historical materialism."[1] Mokyr and I deeply agree with Goldstone, Jacob, and Jones—who together constitute a tiny ideational school of economic history just emerging from the unreflective materialism of our less mature years—that ideas were the steam power of the Great Enrichment.

What Mokyr and I do not *exactly* agree on is whether steam power was its steam power. That is, Mokyr believes that Science was important early, as for example in making it possible for people to imagine atmospheric steam engines once the Scientists had shown that air had weight and that vacuums created by condensing steam could therefore draw a piston in. I believe that if we do the accounting correctly by weighting innovations by their economic importance instead of merely listing them and expressing dazzled admiration, Science does not have much of an economic effect until after about 1900. Most of our riches until then, and quite a few of them down to the present, are the result of technology and technologists, the "tinkerers" you hear so much about (Margaret Jacob detests the word but on the other hand admires the engineers for doing it).

I use the argumentative capitalization of *Science* here because I want to discourage you from using another and dangerous word, much on the popular tongue, *scienceandtechnology*. It is in effect a German portmanteau word, used by Scientists to claim credit for technology, much of which is only remotely connected with their work. High energy physicists at CERN, who should be embarrassed that physics has stagnated for some fifty years (and who therefore, as I have noted, are led to call most of matter and energy "dark"), use scienceandtechnology to keep the billions flowing.[2] (I do not exempt my own beloved science of economics from such hostile characterization, though the amount spent on it is three orders of magnitude below than what is spent on physics or astronomy; if we spent one order of magnitude more on economics we would have such a superior understanding of the causes of economic growth that we could easily finance further studies of elementary particles and manned voyage to Mars). The STEM fields include, too, the M of the mathematicians chiefly interested in Greek-style proofs in number theory or algebraic topology with essentially no applications.

I am not against Science. Let me repeat that. As a reasonable person who for example believes in global warming and actually practices one of the sciences relevant to the evaluation of its causes and solutions, I could hardly be against Science, and am certainly not against plain old science. Mokyr and I are both scientists by anything other than, as I have pointed out, the peculiarly English definition of the past century and a half, during which sense 5b in the *Oxford English Dictionary* became, bizarrely, "the usual sense in ordinary usage," that is, defined as confined to physical and biological "science." (Amusingly, the spouses of both of us have been scientists in the sense 5b.) Thus, Mokyr and I delight in the Dutch word *geesteswetenschappen*, "spirit sciences."

I am merely, as a citizen, against the arrogance of a Science demanding financial support from the rest of us even if it is useless and illiberal, even dangerous. Subsidies to poets would make for faster increases in human welfare than more billions for CERN or the space program. I am merely standing as an economic and historical scientist against Science's claims to account for the whole of the enriched modern world of commercially tested betterment. "Scienceandtechnology" again.

Or to make a slightly different economic point, I am noting (and did also in the book) that Science itself would have little to show if it had not come to be financed massively during the first couple of centuries of the Great Enrichment, sending German boys to study chemistry at the University of Berlin and American boys to study genetics at Iowa State University, and then even the girls. In an illiberal world, further, free inquiry would have been crushed. And the first couple of centuries, down to around 1900, or on a really large scale (penicillin, jet engines) down to around 1950, were attributable mainly to technology, not to the Baconian High Science over which Mokyr so affectingly swoons. Without doubt, as he writes, "German chemists in Giessen developed organic chemistry with enormous effects on industry and agriculture."[3] But *when*, economically speaking, were the "enormous effects"? Unless you think of van Gogh's use of "synthetic lake-of-eosin color," known as geranium lake, as an "enormous effect," the big effect was not until Fritz Haber and artificial fertilizer (and, by the way, poisonous gas in World War I), which indeed was not used enormously until well into the twentieth century. Both the fertilizer and the poison gas. As I said.

Joel claims that "McCloskey simply dismisses the impact of science and the Scientific Revolution as immaterial and of little practical value until 'the 1960s [when] we wanted to navigate our way to the moon.'"[4] Here's what I actually said:

> Francis Bacon, in Mokyr's account, was John the Baptist to the various messiahs of Science, above all Newton. But the messiahs, and even Newton, performed few practical miracles until late in the game—when, for example, in the 1960s we wanted to navigate our way to the moon. The earlier, technologically relevant miracles happened at the lower level among ordinary religionists of a liberal society and therefore of a liberated technology. The Bourgeois Revaluation liberated and dignified ordinary people making betterments.[5]

It makes his case easier to portray me as some sort of *maniak* who dismisses electricity, catalytic cracking, dyestuffs, radio, airplanes, artificial fertilizer, and antibiotics, all of which had heavy inputs from the highest of High Science. I actually said—and I've said it repeatedly to him, in print and in personal correspondence, and indeed in response to an earlier draft of his comments here, which he forthrightly shared with me, though in the end ignoring my replies—that I reckoned that Science started to matter to a considerable part of the economy, as I said, around 1900. That's not the time of the moonshots (though admittedly the shots were the biggest ever application of navigation by Newton's laws of motion).

He says that I "leave out Joseph Priestley, the discoverer of oxygen, the inventor of carbonated drinks and pencil erasers."[6] For one thing, I didn't (for which see page 287). For another, carbonated drinks and pencil erasers make the point against Mokyr's it's-mainly-Science view, namely, that only in a few little corners of the economy did Science much matter until 1900.

Mokyr then falls in with the usual indignant defenses of Science and declares, as though I made such a case, that "the dismissal of any role of formal and codified knowledge in advancing technology and the discourse that led to the triumph of the Baconian program in the West is simply unsupportable."[7] (I thought perhaps he would next accuse me of believing in fairies and astrology, but he refrained.) I never dismissed any role for Science in making us richer. I say to him again: *Lieverd*, what a charge to make! You say 1800, or earlier; I said 1900 or later. It's an empirical matter. Let's go and find out, in a spirit of economic science

Mokyr often in the piece lets his rhetoric get heated in this way for no reason—except the reason, one suspects worryingly, that he is angry that I do not join with sufficient piety the modern worship of Science, which requires that a proper Scientist, he thinks, scorns the humanities. In the sentence claiming that I leave out Priestley, he expresses irritation that I "write at great length about Jane Austen." A proper scientist, if not a Scientist worried about his white coat, would not need to scorn the humanities as a study of categories. But Mokyr has long conveyed to me and others his contempt for the Department of English. I wish he would accept other ways of knowing, first of all by listening to them with his high intelligence fully engaged.

But of course Mokyr, as a great economic historian and a great student of the history of technology, does know better. And so he immediately takes it all back, writing: "McCloskey is of course correct in pointing out that at first the tangible achievements of science were modest. Many scientific areas in which progress would yield its highest fruits in the Great Enrichment turned out to be much messier and more complex than expected. The hopes that 18th-century post-Newton scientists had to Newtonize chemistry, medicine, biology, and agricultural science were all disappointed in the short run."[8] I couldn't have, and didn't, say it better myself, nor did I know the excellent quotation he then gives from Samuel Johnson illustrating the point, in the style of the Department of English, cursed be its name.

Yet he goes off the rails once more: "an economist will remain dissatis-
fied: what is the true driver in this model? Why and how did the discourse
change and the 'Bourgeois Revaluation' prevail in Northwestern Europe
in the 16th and 17th centuries? Why not elsewhere, or at some other
time?"[9] I reply, Good Lord, *gekkie*: I give masses of evidence answering
the very questions. More broadly, the brief quotations he gives of the an-
swers I give are grossly unrepresentative of my argument. My argument
is *backed* by hundreds of pages of documentation of one sort or another.
The way Mokyr presents it suggests that I make silly but briefly summariz-
able claims that are unsustainable and unsubstantiated.

My actual arguments are unorthodox, true, and seem from the point
of view of the orthodoxy of capital accumulation or institutional accumulation to be crazy and disrespectful of my betters such as Lucas and Acemoglu, North and Greif. Mokyr takes rhetorical advantage of orthodox
opinion. (I say to him, It's a cheap trick, dearie, to appeal to an orthodoxy
that you yourself oppose.) He says in effect, "Everyone *knows* that [such
and such a scientifically dubious claim about economic history, which he
himself admits is dubious, or has himself shown to be dubious] is so. Isn't
it shocking that McCloskey *denies* it?!"

I have elsewhere seen Mokyr admit that the 1830s might be the time
by which Science really started to matter much to the economy. I would
say the 1890s. It's not a great difference, considering that both of us deny
the material causes everyone else thinks are crucial. (As I just said, Mokyr
opposes the orthodoxy.) The way to settle the rather minor scientific dis-
agreement between us, I repeat, is to measure. I've repeatedly suggested
to him in correspondence how one might go about it using random sam-
ples of economic activity and then carefully thinking through just how
much the insights of Science mattered to each. He has not responded.

But in any case (a point that the economic historian Robert Margo
has made) economists and economic historians after Robert Fogel's calculation of the social saving from railways cannot leave off their labors
by waving at Great Men or Great Inventions or Great Government In-
tervention and declaring angrily to any doubter that the economy was
obviously "based" on them. The "based" metaphor is indeed a metaphor
and needs to be cashed in with calculations about substitutes. That's economics. Otherwise one is led to say, Mariana Mazzucato–style, that the
economy is "based" on carbonated drinks and pencil erasers, because
everyone uses them. Imagine if our carbonated drinks and erasers were
suddenly taken away. Good Lord!

Mokyr says that the Bourgeois Revaluation was important. I invite him to say so forcefully and to acknowledge that the Scientific Revolution on which he focuses was itself made wide and fruitful by a liberalism that allowed poor people to have a go—ordinary children of the working class such as Humphry Davy, Joseph Fourier, and Thomas Edison—not the cliché of "the rise of the bourgeoisie" or even his scientific or technical elite that mysteriously "arises" without political or social or ethical support.

* * *

In short, we have substantial agreement here. Everyone from Lachmann through Gauss, Baker, Goldstone, Amadae, and Mokyr agrees that ideas mattered, greatly, and in particular the liberal idea making for the technical and scientific and institutional ideas.

The agreement signals a novel scientific advance—or it would be novel, to tell the truth, if it were not in fact the merest commonplace of eighteenth-century liberal thought. The thoughts of the clerisy in the nineteenth century, by contrast, were novel and became commonplaces but were mostly erroneous and regularly evil. Nationalism and socialism were chief among them (and if you like these, perhaps you also will like national socialism), but they ranged from scientific racism and geographic determinism to the rule of arrogant experts. Yet the Great Enrichment itself proved scientifically that, among the erroneous theories, both social Darwinism and economic Marxism were mistaken. The genetically inferior races and classes and ethnicities, contrary to Ernst Haeckel then and Donald Trump now, proved not to be so. They proved to be creative. The exploited proletariat, contrary to Marx then and Bernie Sanders now, was not immiserized. It was enriched.

In the enthusiasm for the materialist but deeply erroneous pseudodiscoveries of the nineteenth century, much of the clerisy mislaid its earlier ideational commitment to a free and dignified common people. It forgot the main, and the one scientifically proven, social discovery of the nineteenth century—a discovery of ur-humanomics, itself in accord with a Romanticism sadly mischievous in other ways—that ordinary men and women do not need to be directed from above. No pushing around. Liberalism. When honored and left alone as autonomous adults they become immensely creative. "I contain multitudes," sang the democratic American poet Walt Whitman. And he, and we, did.

Thus the scientific fruit of humanomics.

Notes

Preface

1. DeMartino 2011; DeMartino and McCloskey 2016.
2. Rorty 1983, 562.
3. Lavoie 1990.
4. Smith and Wilson 2019.
5. For which see McCloskey and Mingardi (2020).
6. Feynman 1974.

Chapter One

1. Coase and Wang 2013, p. 206.
2. https://www.fadedpage.com/books/20120913/html.php. I thank Simon Taylor for the citation.
3. Wilson 1997.
4. Machlup 1978, 250. He was talking this way in the 1940s.
5. Goethe 1963, lines 111–12.
6. Goethe, p. 95.
7. McCloskey 1990.
8. Walras (1874) 1954, 47.
9. On the statistics, see Wasserstein and Lazar (2016), attacking null-hypothesis testing lacking loss functions and substantive measures of importance.
10. Jacobs 1984 (1985), p. 230.

Chapter Two

1. Smith (1762–1763) 1978, chap. vi, para. 56, p. 35.
2. McCloskey 2007.

3. V. Smith 2008, publisher's blurb.

4. Smith (1762–1763) 1978, 352.

5. Smith, 352.

6. Smith (1776) 1981, bk. 1, chap. 2, para. 2, my emphasis.

7. Smith (1762–1763) 1978, 25n3.

8. Robertson 1956, 154.

9. Klamer and McCloskey 1995; McCloskey 2016a, chap. 51; and chapter 6 here. By the way, that our original title referred to one quarter of *GDP*, was a slipup. It is one-quarter of the *labor* income portion of GDP—about 60 percent of GDP—though the other part, especially in its incomes of entrepreneurs of a new hair salon or a new factory, also runs on sweet talk, and probably more than a quarter of the earnings.

10. Banfield 1958, 83–84.

11. Ostrom, Gardner, and Walker, 1994.

12. Hobbes 1914, chap. 14, p. 71.

13. DeMartino 2011.

14. Macaulay (1963), discussed in McCloskey (2006), 129.

15. Frank 2014, p. 20.

16. Mehta 1993.

17. Studied in McCloskey (1990), when I was just beginning to be seriously aware of Austrian economics, though the point was made also by the finance economists at Chicago such as Merton Miller and Fischer Black, with whom I lunched daily in the 1970s, and was anyway a commonplace among some humanists, such as Alasdair McIntyre, whom I studied in the 1980s at the University of Iowa.

Chapter Three

1. Sutch 1991.

2. Williamson 1974; Gerschenkron 1970.

3. And in some of the little critical essays in McCloskey (2020), such as essays on Kennedy, and on the matter of general-equilibrium simulation, the essay on Williamson.

4. Arrow 1960; Wasserstein and Lazar 2016; Ziliak and McCloskey 2008.

Chapter Four

1. Pope 1711, *Essay on Criticism*, lines 221–224.

2. Tirole 2006.

3. Pearson and Moul 1925; Pearson (1892) 1900, 26–28.

4. Leonard 2016. Buck v. Bell, 274 U.S. 200 (1927). The Virginia law in question

was on the books until 1974, which is also when similar laws in Sweden and Norway were overturned.

5. Quoted in McEvoy (2001), 291. The provenance of the remark is a little hazy, but it is well known. In Danish, the philosopher Hans Siggaard Jensen informs me, it was something like "Fysik er ikke om hvordan verden er, men om hvad vi kan sige om den."

6. Ausländer. *Gedichte von Rose Ausländer*: "Am Anfang /war das Wort / und das Wort / war bei Gott / Und Gott gab uns das Wort / und wir wohnten / im Wort / Und das Wort ist unser Traum / und der Traum ist unser Leben."

7. Stevens 1934.

8. For which see McCloskey (2018) on Robert Skidelsky's Keynesian revival of the idea and McCloskey and Mingardi (2020) on Marianna Mazzucato's application in 2013 of the idea to policy about innovation.

9. Keynes 1936, chap. 12, sec. 8.

10. Diamond (1988), though Leland Yeager (1999) noted correctly that it does provide a useful "integrating factor of the whole body of economic theory" (28).

11. Lazonick 1991.

12. McCloskey 2016a, chaps. 27–28, 32–33.

Chapter Five

1. Whaples 2010.

2. Olmstead and Rhode 2018.

3. Kelvin (1883) 1888–1889, italics in source. Note the sense 5b use of "science."

4. Quoted in Merton, Sills, and Stigler (1984). I thank Ross Emmett for setting me straight on this.

5. An example of the anger is Hoover and Sigler (2008) on statistical significance.

6. The other is the hero Jim Dixon in Kingsley Amis's *Lucky Jim* (1954).

7. Ibsen (1891) 1965, act 2. The other economic historian in literature is the hero in Kingsley Amis's *Lucky Jim* (1954).

Chapter Six

1. Advertising expenditure data set VI.1, http://spreadsheets.google.com/pib? key=p91LENaiKJeoyBX4eR1FZEEw (no longer posted). For advertising and for nominal income, see http://data360.org/dataset.aspx?Data_Set_Id=352.

2. *Statistical Abstract of the United States 2007*, http://census.gov/compendia /statab/2007/2007edition.html (no longer posted).

3. Lodge 1990, 219.

4. Klamer and McCloskey 1995.

5. Antioch 2013, table 3.

6. Wallis and North 1986, table 3.13.

7. Bureau of Census, *Statistical Abstract of the United States 2006* (Washington, DC: Government Printing Office, 2006), table 650, p. 430; and Johnston 2012.

8. Pink 2012, 21.

9. Pink, 6.

Chapter Seven

1. For example, Klamer 2011; Amariglio and McCloskey 2008.

2. Lachmann 1950.

3. For a thorough exploration of the metaphor and the story of the prisoner's dilemma in its relation to political theory, see the dissertation in progress at the Department of Political Science at the University of Chicago by Alfred Saucedo.

4. Michael C. Jensen is an example of toppling (McCloskey 2017).

5. Lachmann 1978.

6. A full treatment of virtue ethics in an economic context is McCloskey (2006), but while I was off in Amsterdam ruminating on the subject, a large team of "positive psychologists" under the auspices of the American Psychological Association came to similar conclusions (Peterson and Seligman 2004). But St. Thomas Aquinas in 1270 had scooped us all.

7. See the account of the "cognitive revolution" in Bruner (1983) and Kagan (2006). For economic experiments with animals, see Battalio and Kagel (1975, 1981).

8. Hart 2013, 156, 161.

9. Lachmann 1971, 49.

10. Lachmann, 61.

11. Lachmann, 63–64.

12. Lachmann, 67.

13. Rubin 2017.

14. Lachmann 1971, 74.

15. Searle 2010.

16. Viner (1950) 1991.

Chapter Eight

1. Segrè and Hoerlin 2016, 272–73.

2. Lachmann 1977, quoted in Boettke and Storr 2002, 171.

3. Butler (1725) 1736, preface, 349.

4. Grotius 1625, propositions 6 and 7.

5. Lachmann 1977, quoted in Boettke and Storr 2002, 171; North 1990, 2005.

6. The question was suggested at the Sunday Seminar at my house by my friend Laurence Iannaccone of Chapman University.

7. Kant A50–51/B74–76, quoted in Hanna 2017.

8. Lachmann 1976b, quoted in Dolan 1976, 149.

9. Lachmann 1976c, quoted in Dolan 1976, 157–58.

10. Lachmann 1976a, quoted in Dolan 1976, 216, italics added.

11. Lachmann 1976a, quoted in Dolan 1976, 217.

12. Lachmann 1976a, quoted in Dolan 1976, 218.

Chapter Nine

1. Bresson 2016, 205.

2. McCloskey 2011.

3. Keynes 1936, 16.

4. Smith (1776) 1981, 4.9.51.

5. LaVaque-Manty 2006, 715–16.

6. Compare the only slightly less sweeping language in 1789 of the (first) French *Declaration of the Rights of Man and of the Citizen*, art. 1: "Men are born and remain free and equal in rights. Social distinctions may be founded only upon the general good."

7. LaVaque-Manty 2006, 716.

8. Ibsen (1877) 1965, 30.

9. Thucydides bk. 1, translated at University of Minnesota Human Rights Library, http://www1.umn.edu/humanrts/education/thucydides.html.

10. See White 1984, citing Thucydides, 3.3.82–84.

11. Neal and Williamson, eds. 2014, p. 2.

Chapter Ten

1. Arendt (1951) 1985, 56, 62.

2. Aristotle 1968, 1.1254a.

3. Moynahan 2002, 541.

4. David Friedman made the point in a blog reacting to *Bourgeois Dignity* (McCloskey 2010), July 17, 2013, https://daviddfriedman.blogspot.com/2013/07/.

5. Charles's speech is given at Project Canterbury ("Printed by Peter Cole, at the sign of the Printing-Press in Cornhil, near the Royal Exchange"), http://anglicanhistory.org/charles/charles1.html. In the document the year is given as 1648, because in the Julian calendar the year did not begin until March. So it is a Julian date in a New Style year.

6. Quoted in Brailsford (1961), 624.

7. Rumbold (1685) 1961.

8. From the King's *Memoires*, 63, widely quoted, as in Keohane (1980), 248n18.

9. Overton (1646) 2014.

10. Blainey 2009, 272.

11. Mencken 1916.

12. Mencken 1949, 622.

13. As, among others, Sheri Berman (2006) has argued.

14. Reprinted and translated in Horst (1996), 142. The poem was called "Liefdesverklaring," or "Love-Declaration."

15. Personal communication, 2014.

16. Yeats (1928) 1992, 260.

Chapter Eleven

1. Mueller 2011, 1.

2. Lal 1998; summarized in Lal 2006, 5, 155.

3. Needham 1954–2008; Pomeranz 2000; and others.

4. Taylor 1989, 23; 2007, 179.

5. Jacob 2001.

6. Parks 2005, 180.

7. Harkness 2008.

8. Danford 2006, 319.

9. The quotation from Lord Kames (1774) is Danford's.

10. Danford 2006, 324.

11. Danford 2006, 331.

12. Danford 2006, xxx.

13. Hume (1741–1742) 1987, "Of Commerce."

14. See Palmer 2014.

15. Ringmar 2007, 31.

16. Ringmar 2007, 32.

17. Ringmar 2007, 24. Ringmar's remarkable literacy in an English not his native tongue, by the way, shows in his accurate use of the phrase "begs the question," which is widely but mistakenly understood to mean "suggests the question." It means inserting your conclusion into your premise, circular reasoning, *petitiio principii.*

18. Jones 2010, 102–3.

19. Ringmar 2007, 250, 254, 274, 279, 280–282.

20. Ogilvie 2007, 662–63.

21. Ringmar 2007, 72, 178, 286.

22. Ringmar 2007, 37.

23. Le Bris 2013.

24. Kennedy 1976, 59.
25. Kadane 2008.
26. Thomson 2005.
27. Sprat (1667) 1958, 88.
28. Dryden (1672) 1994, 2.1.391–93.
29. Child 1698, 68, 148.

Chapter Twelve

1. Clark 2007.
2. Though I readily admit that the forthcoming book by Nick Cowen, Ilia Murtazashvili, Raufhon Salahodjaev, *Individualism and Well-Being* (2021), makes a very good case for individualism, understood as enlightened self-interest, not selfishness, or the "possessive individualism" that haunts the nightmares of the left.
3. Landes 1998, 522.
4. Moore 1998, 148, 151. For an instance in China, see Mote (1999), 335, on the career of the philosopher Chen Liang (1143–1194) in the Southern Song.
5. Moore 1998, 156.
6. Goldstone 1998.
7. North, Wallis, and Weingast 2009, 25.
8. Lawler 2008.
9. M. Smith 1999, 121.
10. Smith (1776) 1981, bk. 1, chap. 4, para. 1.

Chapter Thirteen

1. McCloskey and Carden 2020.
2. Gerschenkron 1962.
3. Davidoff and Hall 1987, 162.
4. Sewell 1994, 198.
5. Tocqueville (1856) 1955, 146–47. I owe this citation to Clifford Deaton.
6. Hughes 1936.
7. Virgil Storr (2012 and his earlier work) makes this point in the context of the economy of Barbados.
8. Lakoff 2020.
9. Higgs 1987.
10. Whitney v. California, 274 U.S. 357 (1927).
11. Ardagh 1991, 297.
12. Landes 1998, 38.
13. Baumol, Litan, and Schramm 2007, 122.

14. Manin 1987, 338.
15. Manin, 364.
16. Harkness 2008.

Chapter Fourteen

1. Gaus 2016; Baker 2016; Amadae 2016; Goldstone 2016; Mokyr 2016.
2. Gaus, 1.
3. Plantinga 2000, xiv. I have in the past, without properly checking the source, improved on his remark by remembering it as "but a tetralogy is an abomination." Thus scribal error.
4. Smith (1776) 1981, bk. 4, chap. 9, para. 3. Smith is here attacking Colbert and mercantilism. Speaking of scribal error, I often get wrong the order Smith gave to the three attributes of an unplanned plan of "allowing every man to pursue his own interest in his own way."
5. Gaus 2016, p. 11.
6. Gaus 2016, 3.
7. McCloskey 2010, chaps. 33–36; 2016a, chaps. 14–15; 2013; 2014a; 2014b; 2015.
8. Gaus 2016, 3.
9. Smith (1762–1766) 1978, A.vi.56.
10. Gaus 2016, 4.
11. Grief 2006.
12. Gaus 2016, 4.
13. Gaus, 11.
14. Gaus, 3.
15. Gaus, 7.
16. Gaus, 6.
17. Gaus, 4.
18. McCloskey 2016a, 235–54.
19. The passage is brilliantly analyzed in White 1984.
20. Gaus 2016, 7.
21. Gintis 2009; Bowles and Gintis 2011; Field 2003.
22. Gaus 2016, 7.
23. Gaus, 7.
24. Gaus, 5.
25. Baker 2016, 27.
26. Baker, 35.
27. Baker, 34.
28. Baker, 34.
29. Baker, 33.
30. Baker, 31.

31. Quoted in Palmer 2012, 35.

32. Baker 2016, 33.

33. Baker, 30.

34. Baker, 34.

35. Baker, 30.

36. Baker, 30.

37. Baker, 31.

38. Baker, 32n8.

39. McCloskey 2016a, 575.

Chapter Fifteen

1. Goldstone 2016, 15.

2. Goldstone, 18.

3. Goldstone, 19.

4. Goldstone, 19.

5. Goldstone, 19–20.

6. Cartwright and Hardie 2012, e.g., p. 100.

7. Goldstone 2016, 18.

8. Findlay and O'Rourke 2007.

9. Goldstone 2016, 22.

10. Goldstone, 23.

11. Zhangi Yi of Zhejiang University in Hangchou, China is writing a brilliant PhD thesis on the matter.

12. Amadae 2016, 38.

13. Amadae, 38.

14. Amadae, 42.

15. Amadae, 42.

16. Amadae, 46.

17. Amadae, 46.

18. I apologize for quoting earlier drafts of her piece, but the point seems important. Amadae was permitted to revise after I had written my reply, which is not how it's supposed to be done.

19. Amadae 2016, 39.

20. Amadae, 39.

21. Amadae, 39.

22. A short form is McCloskey 2016b.

23. Amadae 2016, 40.

24. For example, Olmstead and Rhode 2018.

25. Amadae 2016, 40.

26. McCloskey 2014b.

27. Amadae 2016, 59.
28. Amadae, 50.
29. McCloskey 2016a, 204.
30. Amadae 2016, 50–51.

Chapter Sixteen

1. Mokyr 2016, 55.
2. For which see Horgan 1996.
3. Mokyr 2016, 58.
4. Mokyr, 56.
5. McCloskey 2016a, 506. I do admit to having a distaste for Francis Bacon, who was the last man in England to use torture for official purposes and who, when he rose to Lord Chancellor, sold decisions in legal cases, to both sides, and was caught.
6. Mokyr 2016, 58.
7. Mokyr, 57.
8. Mokyr, 60.
9. Mokyr, 61.

Works Cited

Akerlof, George A. 1970. "The Market for 'Lemons': Quality Uncertainty and the Market Mechanism." *Quarterly Journal of Economics* 84:488–500.

Amadae, Sonja M. 2016. "Dialectical Libertarianism: The Unintended Consequences of Both Ethics and Incentives Underlie Mutual Prosperity." *Erasmus Journal for Philosophy and Economic* 9 (2): 27–52. http://ejpe.org/pdf/9-2-art-4.pdf.

Amariglio, Jack, with Deirdre Nansen McCloskey. 2008. "Fleeing Capitalism: A Slightly Disputatious Conversation/Interview among Friends." In *Sublime Economy: On the Intersection of Art and Economics*, edited by Jack Amariglio, Joseph Childers, and Steven Cullenberg, 276–319. London: Routledge.

Antioch, Gerry. 2013. "Persuasion Is Now 30 Per Cent of US GDP." In *Economic Roundup*, vol. 1, Australian Treasury, 1–10. http://ideas.repec.org/a/tsy/journl/journl_tsy_er_2013_1_1.html.

Aquinas, St. Thomas. 1984. *Treatise on the Virtues*. Translated and edited by John A. Oesterle. Notre Dame, IN: University of Notre Dame Press.

Ardagh, John. 1991. *Germany and the Germans*. Rev. ed. London: Penguin.

Arendt, Hannah. (1951) 1985. *The Origins of Modern Totalitarianism*. New ed. New York: Harcourt.

Aristotle. 1968. *Aristotle's Politics*. Edited by E. Baker. Oxford: Oxford University Press.

Arrow, Kenneth J. 1960. "Decision Theory and the Choice of a Level of Significance for the *t*-Test." In *Contributions to Probability and Statistics: Essays in Honor of Harold Hotelling*, edited by Ingram Olkin et al., 70–78. Stanford, CA: Stanford University Press.

Ausländer, Rose. *Gedichte von Rose Ausländer*. http://www.deanita.de/buecher19.htm.

Baker, Jennifer. 2016. "A Place at the Table: Low Wage Workers and the Bourgeois Deal." *Erasmus Journal for Philosophy and Economics* 9 (2): 25–36.
http://ejpe.org/pdf/9-2-art-3.pdf.

Banfield, Edward C. 1958. *The Moral Basis of a Backward Society*. New York:
Free Press.

Battalio, R. C., and John Kagel. 1975. "Experimental Studies of Consumer Demand Behavior Using Laboratory Animals," *Economic Inquiry* 13 (March):
22–38.

Battalio, R. C., and John Kagel. 1981. "Commodity Choice Behavior with Pigeons
as Subjects." *Journal of Political Economy* 89:67–91.

Baumol, William, Robert E. Litan, and Carl J. Schramm. 2007. *Good Capitalism,
Bad Capitalism, and the Economics of Growth and Prosperity*. New Haven, CT:
Yale University Press.

Berman, Harold J. 2003. *Law and Revolution, II: The Impact of the Protestant Ref-
ormations on the Western Legal Tradition*. Cambridge, MA: Harvard University Press.

Berman, Sheri. 2006. *The Primacy of Politics: Social Democracy and the Making of
Europe's Twentieth Century*. Cambridge: Cambridge University Press.

Blainey, Geoffrey. 2009. *A Shorter History of Australia*. North Sydney: Random
House Australia.

Boettke, Peter J., and Virgil Henry Storr. 2002. "Post Classical Political Economy."
American Journal of Economics and Sociology 61 (1): 161–91.

Bowles, Samuel, and Herbert Gintis. 2011. *A Cooperative Species: Human Social-
ity and Its Evolution*. Princeton, NJ: Princeton University Press.

Brailsford, H. E. 1961. *The Levellers and the English Revolution*. Stanford, CA:
Stanford University Press.

Bresson, Alain . 2016. *The Making of the Ancient Greek Economy: Institutions,
Markets, and Growth in the City States*. Translated by Steven Rendall. Chicago:
University of Chicago Press.

Bruner, Jerome. 1983. *In Search of Mind: Essays in Autobiography*. New York:
Harper and Row.

Butler, Joseph, Bishop. (1725) 1736. *Fifteen Sermons*. In *The Analogy of Religion
and Fifteen Sermons*, 3rd ed., 335–528. London.

Cartwright, Nancy, and Jeremy Hardie. 2012. *Evidence-Based Policy: A Practical
Guide to Doing It Better*. New York: Oxford University Press.

Child, Josiah. 1698. *A New Discourse of Trade*. London.

Clark, Gregory. 2007. *A Farewell to Alms: A Brief Economic History of the World*.
Princeton, NJ: Princeton University Press.

Coase, Ronald, and Ning Wang. 2013. *How China Became Capitalist*. Basingstoke:
Palgrave-Macmillan.

Cowen Nick, Ilia Murtazashvili, and Raufhon Salahodjaev. 2021. *Individualism
and Well-Being* Brighton: Edward Arnold.

Danford, John W. 2006. " 'Riches Valuable at All Times and to All Men': Hume and the Eighteenth-Century Debate on Commerce and Liberty." In *Liberty and American Experience in the Eighteenth Century*, edited by David Womersley, 319–47. Indianapolis, IN: Liberty Fund.

Davidoff, Leonore, and Catherine Hall. 1987. *Family Fortunes: Men and Women of the English Middle Class, 1780–1850*. Chicago: University of Chicago Press.

DeMartino, George F. 2011. *The Economist's Oath: On the Need for and Content of Professional Economic Ethics*. New York: Oxford.

DeMartino, George F., and Deirdre Nansen McCloskey, eds. 2016. *The Oxford Handbook of Professional Economic Ethics*. New York: Oxford University Press.

Diamond, Arthur M., Jr. 1988. "The Empirical Progressiveness of the General Equilibrium Research Program." *History of Political Economy* 20, no. 1 (Spring): 119–35.

Dolan, Edwin, ed., 1976. *The Foundations of Modern Austrian Economics*. Kansas City: Sheed and Ward.

Dryden, John. (1672) 1994. *Amboyna*. In *The Works of John Dryden*, vol. 12, edited by V. A. Dearing. Berkeley: University of California Press.

Feynman, Richard. P 1974. "Cargo Cult Science: Some Remarks on Science, Pseudoscience, and Learning How to Not Fool Yourself" (commencement address at Caltech). *Engineering and Science* 37 (7), http://calteches.library.caltech.edu/51/2/CargoCult.pdf.

Field, Alexander. 2003. *Altruistically Inclined? The Behavioral Sciences, Evolutionary Theory, and the Origins of Reciprocity*. Ann Arbor: University of Michigan Press.

Findlay, Ronald, and Kevin H. O'Rourke. 2007. *Power and Plenty: Trade, War, and the World Economy in the Second Millennium*. Princeton, NJ: Princeton University Press.

Frank, Robert H. 2014. *What Price the Moral High Ground? How to Succeed without Selling Your Soul*. Princeton, NJ: Princeton University Press.

Gaus, Gerald. 2016. "The Open Society as a Rule-Based Order." *Erasmus Journal for Philosophy and Economics* 9 (2): 1–13. http://ejpe.org/pdf/9-2-art-1.pdf.

Gerschenkron, Alexander. 1962. "Reflections on the Concept of 'Prerequisites' of Modern Industrialization." In *Economic Backwardness in Historical Perspective: A Book of Essays*, 31–51. Cambridge, MA: Harvard University Press.

Gerschenkron, Alexander. 1970. *Europe in the Russian Mirror: Four Essays in Economic History*. Cambridge: Cambridge University Press.

Gintis, Herbert. 2009. *The Bounds of Reason: Game Theory and the Unification of the Behavioral Sciences*. Princeton, NJ: Princeton University Press.

Goethe, Johann Wolfgang von. 1963. *Goethe's Faust: Part 1 and Sections of Part 2*. Translated by Walter Kaufman. Garden City, NY: Anchor.

Goffman, Erving. 1961. *Asylums: Essays on the Social Situation of Mental Patients and Other Inmates*. New York: Doubleday.

Goldstone, Jack A. 1998. "The Problem of the 'Early Modern' World." *Journal of the Economic and Social History of the Orient* 41:249–84.

Goldstone, Jack A. 2002. "Efflorescences and Economic Growth in World History: Rethinking the 'Rise of the West' and the Industrial Revolution." *Journal of World History* 13:323–89.

Goldstone, Jack A. 2016. "Either/Or: Why Ideas, Science, Imperialism, and Institutions All Matter in 'The Rise of the West.'" *Erasmus Journal for Philosophy and Economics* 9 (2) 14–24. http://ejpe.org/pdf/9-2-art-2.pdf.

Greif, Avner. 2006. *Institutions and the Path to the Modern Economy: Lessons from Medieval Trade*. Cambridge: Cambridge University Press.

Grotius [Hugo de Groot]. 1625. "Preliminary Discourse concerning the Certainty of Rights in General." In *De iure belli ac pacis*. English trans. of 1738, from the French of Jean Barbeyrac, 1720.

Hanna, Robert. 2017. "The Togetherness Principle, Kant's Conceptualism, and Kant's Non-Conceptualism." Supplement to "Kant's Theory of Judgement *Stanford Encyclopedia of Philosophy*. https://plato.stanford.edu/entries/kant-judgment/supplement1.html.

Harkness, D. 2008. "Accounting for Science: How a Merchant Kept His Books in Elizabethan London." In *The Self-Perception of Early Modern Capitalists*, edited by Margaret C. Jacob and Catherine Secretan, 205–28). New York: Palgrave Macmillan.

Hart, David Bentley. 2013. *The Experience of God: Being, Consciousness, Bliss*. New Haven, CT: Yale University Press.

Hayek, Friedrich A., ed. 1954. *Capitalism and the Historians: Essays by Hayek, T. S. Ashton, L. M. Hacker, W. H. Hutt, and B. de Jouvenel*. Chicago: University of Chicago Press.

Higgs, Robert. 1987. *Crisis and Leviathan: Critical Episodes in the Growth of American Government*. New York: Oxford University Press.

Hobbes, Thomas. 1914. *Leviathan*. Everyman Edition. London: J. M. Dent.

Hoover, Kevin, and Mark Siegler. 2008. "Sound and Fury: McCloskey and Significance Testing in Economics." *Journal of Economic Methodology* 15:1–37.

Horgan, John. 1996. *The End of Science: Facing the Limits of Science in the Twilight of the Scientific Age*. New York: Broadway Books.

Horst, H. 1996. *The Low Sky: Understanding the Dutch*. Schiedam: Scriptum.

Hughes, Langston. 1936. "Let America Be America Again." https://poets.org/poem/let-america-be-america-again.

Hume, David. (1741–1742) 1987. *Essays, Moral, Political and Literary*. Edited by E. F. Miller. Indianapolis, IN: Liberty Fund.

Ibsen, Henrik. (1877) 1965. *The Enemy of the People*. In *Ibsen: The Complete Major Prose and Plays*, translated and edited by R. Fjelde. New York: Penguin.

Ibsen, Henrik. (1891) 1965. *Hedda Gabler*. In *Ibsen: The Complete Major Prose and Plays*, translated and edited by R. Fjelde. New York: Penguin.

Ibsen, Henrik. 1965. *Ibsen: The Complete Major Prose and Plays*. Translated and edited by R. Fjelde. New York: Penguin.

Jacob, Margaret C. 2001. *The Enlightenment: A Brief History*. Boston: Bedford/St. Martin's.

Jacobs, Jane. 1985. *Cities and the Wealth of Nations: Principles of Economic Life*. New York: Vintage.

Jacobs, Jane. 1992. *Systems of Survival: A Dialogue on the Moral Foundations of Commerce and Politics*. New York: Random House.

Johnston, Louis D. 2012. "History Lessons: Understanding the Decline in Manufacturing." *MinnPost*, February 12. http://minnpost.com/macro-micro-minnesota/2012/02/history-lessons-understanding-decline-manufacturing.

Jones, Eric L. 2010. *Locating the Industrial Revolution: Inducement and Response*. London: World Scientific.

Kadane, Matthew. 2008. "Success and Self-Loathing in the Life of an Eighteenth-Century Entrepreneur." In *The Self-Perception of Early Modern Capitalists*, edited by Margaret C. Jacob and Catherine Secretan, 253–71. New York: Palgrave Macmillan.

Kagan, Jerome. 2006. *An Argument for Mind*. New Haven, CT: Yale University Press.

Kelvin, William Thompson, Lord. (1883) 1899–1889. "Electrical Units of Measurement." Reprinted in *Popular Lectures and Addresses*, vol. 1. London.

Kennedy, Paul M. 1976. *The Rise and Fall of British Naval Mastery*. New York: Scribner's.

Keohane, Nannerl O. 1980. *Philosophy and the State in France: The Renaissance to the Enlightenment*. Princeton, NJ: Princeton University Press.

Keynes, John Maynard. 1936. *The General Theory of Employment, Interest and Money*. London: Macmillan.

Klamer, Arjo, and Deirdre Nansen McCloskey. 1995. "One Quarter of GDP Is Persuasion." *American Economic Review* 85:191–95.

Klamer, Arjo. 2011. "Cultural Entrepreneurship." *Review of Austrian Economics* 24:141–56.

Lachmann, Ludwig M. 1950. "Economics as a Social Science." *South African Journal of Economics* 18: 215–18.

Lachmann, Ludwig M. 1971. *The Legacy of Max Weber*. Berkeley: Glendessary Press.

Lachmann, Ludwig M. 1976a. "Austrian Economics in the Age of the Neo-Ricardian Counterrevolution." In *The Foundations of Modern Austrian Economics*, edited by Edwin Dolan, 215–23. Kansas City: Sheed and Ward.

Lachmann, Ludwig M. 1976b "On Austrian Capital Theory." In *The Foundations of Modern Austrian Economics*, edited by Edwin Dolan, 145–51. Kansas City: Sheed and Ward.

Lachmann, Ludwig M. 1976c. "Toward a Critique of Macroeconomics." In *The Foundations of Modern Austrian Economics*, edited by Edwin Dolan, 152–59. Kansas City: Sheed and Ward.

Lachmann, Ludwig M. 1978. "An Interview with Ludwig Lachmann." *Austrian Economics Newsletter* 1, no. 3 (Fall). https://mises.org/library/interview -ludwig-lachmann.

Lakoff, George. 2020. *Moral Politics: How Liberals and Conservatives Think.* 2nd ed. Chicago: University of Chicago Press.

Lal, Deepak. 1998. *Unintended Consequences: The Impact of Factor Endowments, Culture, and Politics on Long-Run Economic Performance.* Cambridge, MA: MIT Press.

Lal, Deepak. 2006. *Reviving the Invisible Hand: The Case for Classical Liberalism in the Twentieth Century.* Princeton, NJ: Princeton University Press.

Landes, David S. 1998. *The Wealth and Poverty of Nations: Why Some Are So Rich and Some So Poor.* New York: W. W. Norton.

LaVaque-Manty, Mika. 2006." Dueling for Equality: Masculine Honor and the Modern Politics of Dignity." *Political Theory* 34:715–40.

Lavoie, Don C. 1990. Introduction to *Economics and Hermeneutics*, 1–18. London: Routledge.

Lawler, Andrew. 2008. "Boring No More, a Trade-Savvy Indus Emerges." *Science* 320, no. 5881: 1276–81.

Lazonick, William. 1991. "Business History and Economics." *Business and Economic History* 2nd ser., 20:1–13.

Le Bris, David. 2013. "Customary versus Civil Law within Old Regime France." KEDGE Business School, MPRA paper no. 521232013. http://mpra.ub.uni -muenchen.de/52123/1/MPRA_paper_52123.pdf.

Leonard, Thomas C. 2016. *Illiberal Reformers: Race, Eugenics, and American Economics in the Progressive Era.* Princeton, NJ: Princeton University Press.

Lodge, David. 1990. *Nice Work.* London: Penguin.

Macaulay, Stewart. 1963. "Non-contractual Relations in Business." *American Sociological Review* 28: 55–67. Reprinted in *The Sociology of Economic Life*, edited by Mark Granovetter and Richard Swedberg, 191–205. Boulder: Westview, 2016.

Machlup, Fritz. 1978. *Methodology of Economics and Other Social Sciences.* New York: Academic.

Manin, Bernard. 1987. "On Legitimacy and Political Deliberation." Translated by Elly Stein and Jane Mansbridge. *Political Theory* 15: 338–68.

Marschak, Jacob. 1968. "Economics of Inquiring, Communicating, Deciding." *American Economic Review* 58 (May): 1–18.

Mazzucato, Mariana. 2013. *The Entrepreneurial State: Debunking Public vs. Private Sector Myths.* London: Anthem Press.

McCloskey, Deirdre Nansen. (1985) 1998. *The Rhetoric of Economics.* 2nd ed. Madison: University of Wisconsin Press.

McCloskey, Deirdre Nansen. 1990. *If You're So Smart: The Narrative of Economic Expertise.* Chicago: University of Chicago Press.

McCloskey, Deirdre Nansen. 1994a. "Bourgeois Virtue." *American Scholar* 63, no. 2 (Spring): 177–91.

McCloskey, Deirdre Nansen. 1994b. *Knowledge and Persuasion in Economics.* Cambridge: Cambridge University Press.

McCloskey, Deirdre Nansen. 2006. *The Bourgeois Virtues: Ethics for an Age of Commerce.* Chicago: University of Chicago Press.

McCloskey, Deirdre Nansen. 2007. "A Solution to the Alleged Inconsistency in the Neoclassical Theory of Markets: Reply to Guerrien's Reply." *Post-Autistic Economics Review* (September 18).

McCloskey, Deirdre Nansen. 2010. *Bourgeois Dignity: Why Economics Can't Explain the Modern World.* Chicago: University of Chicago Press.

McCloskey, Deirdre Nansen. 2011. "The Prehistory of American Thrift." In *Thrift and Thriving in America: Capitalism and Moral Order from the Puritans to the Present,* edited by Joshua J. Yates and James Davidson Hunter, 61–87. New York: Oxford University Press, 2011.

McCloskey, Deirdre Nansen. 2013. "A Neo-Institutionalism of Measurement, Without Measurement: A Comment on Douglas Allen's *The Institutional Revolution.*" *Review of Austrian Economics* 26 (4): 262–373.

McCloskey, Deirdre Nansen. 2014a. "Getting Beyond Neo-Institutionalism: Virgil Storr's Culture of Markets." *Review of Austrian Economics* 27:463–72.

McCloskey, Deirdre Nansen. 2014b. "Measured, Unmeasured, Mismeasured, and Unjustified Pessimism: A Review Essay of Thomas Piketty's *Capital in the Twenty-First Century.*" *Erasmus Journal for Philosophy and Economics* 7:73–115.

McCloskey, Deirdre Nansen. 2015. "Max U versus Humanomics: A Critique of Neo-Institutionalism." *Journal of Institutional Economics* 12:1–27.

McCloskey, Deirdre Nansen. 2016a. *Bourgeois Equality: How Ideas, Not Capital or Institutions, Enriched the World.* Chicago: University of Chicago Press.

McCloskey, Deirdre Nansen. 2016b. "Economic Liberty as Anti-flourishing: Marx and Especially His Followers." In *Economic Liberty and Human Flourishing: Perspectives from Political Philosophy,* edited by Michael R. Strain and Stan A. Veuger, 129–49. Washington, DC: American Enterprise Institute.

McCloskey, Deirdre Nansen. 2017. "Comment on 'Putting Integrity into Finance: A Purely Positive Approach' (by Werner Erhard and Michael C. Jensen)." *Capitalism and Society* 12:1–12.

McCloskey, Deirdre Nansen. 2018. "Review of Robert Skidelsky's *Money and Government:* Please Don't Call It Socialism." *Wall Street Journal,* December 5.

McCloskey, Deirdre Nansen. 2019. *Why Liberalism Works: How True Liberal Values Produce a Freer, More Equal, Prosperous World for All.* New Haven: Yale University Press.

McCloskey, Deirdre Nansen. 2020. *Historical Impromptus: Notes, Reviews, and Responses on the British Experience and the Great Enrichment.* Great Barrington, MA: American Institute for Economic Research.

McCloskey, Deirdre Nansen, and Art Carden. 2020. *Leave Me Alone and I'll Make You Rich: How the Bourgeois Deal Enriched the World*. Chicago: University of Chicago Press.

McCloskey, Deirdre Nansen, and Alberto Mingardi. 2020. *The Illiberal Myth of the Entrepreneurial State*. London: Adam Smith Institute; Great Barrington, MA: American Institute for Economic Research.

McCloskey, Deirdre Nansen. 2021. *Economic Impromptus: Notes, Reviews, and Responses on Economics*. Great Barrington, MA: American Institute for Economic Research.

McEvoy, Paul, ed. 2001. *Niels Bohr: Reflections on Subject and Object*. San Francisco: Microanalytix, 2001.

Mehta, Judith. 1993. "Meaning in the Context of Bargaining Games: Narratives in Opposition." In *Economics and Language*, edited by Willie Henderson, Tony Dudley-Evans, and Roger Backhouse, 85–99. London: Routledge.

Mencken, H. L. 1916. *A Little Book in C Major*. New York: John Lane.

Mencken, H. L. 1949. *A Mencken Chrestomathy: His Own Selection of His Choicest Writing*. New York: Knopf.

Merton, Robert K., David L. Sills, and Stephen M. Stigler. 1984. "The Kelvin Dictum and Social Science: An Excursion into the History of an Idea." *Journal of the History of the Behavioral Sciences* 20:319–31.

Mokyr, Joel. 2016. "The Bourgeoisie and the Scholar." *Erasmus Journal for Philosophy and Economics* 9 (2): 55–65. https://doi.org/10.23941/ejpe.v9i2.229.

Moore, Barrington. 1998. "Rational Discussion: Comparative Historical Notes on Its Origins, Enemies, and Prospects." *Moral Aspects of Economic Growth and Other Essays*, 144–57. Ithaca, NY: Cornell University Press.

Mote, F. W. 1999. *Imperial China, 900–1800*. Cambridge, MA: Harvard University Press.

Moynahan, Brian. 2002. *The Faith: A History of Christianity*. New York: Doubleday.

Mueller, John. 2011. *War and Ideas: Selected Essays*. New York: Routledge.

Neal, Larry, Jeffrey G. Williamson., eds. 2014. *The Cambridge History of Capitalism*, vol. 1, *The Rise of Capitalism from Ancient Origins to 1848*. Cambridge: Cambridge University Press.

Needham, Joseph. 1954–2008. *Science and Civilization in China*. 27 vols. Cambridge: Cambridge University Press.

North, Douglass C. 1990. *Institutions, Institutional Change and Economic Performance*. Cambridge: Cambridge University Press.

North, Douglass C. 2005. *Understanding the Process of Economic Change*. Princeton Economic History of the Western World. Princeton, NJ: Princeton University Press.

North, Douglass C., John Joseph Wallis, and Barry R. Weingast. 2009. *Violence and Social Orders: A Conceptual Framework for Interpreting Recorded Human History*. Cambridge: Cambridge University Press.

Ogilvie, Sheilagh. 2007. "'Whatever Is, Is Right'? Economic Institutions in Preindustrial Europe. *Economic History Review* 60:649–84.

Olmstead, Alan L., and Paul W. Rhode. 2018. "Cotton, Slavery, and the New History of Capitalism." *Explorations in Economic History* 67:1–17.

Ostrom, Eleanor, Roy Gardner, and J. Walker. 1994. *Rules, Games, and Common-Pool Resources.* Ann Arbor: University of Michigan Press.

Overton, Richard. (1646) 2014. *An Arrow against All Tyrants.* Vol. 3 of *Tracts on Liberty by the Levellers and their Critics*, edited by David M. Hart. Indianapolis: Liberty Fund.

Palmer, Tom G. 2012. "Bismarck's Legacy," In *After the Welfare State: Politicians Stole Your Future, You Can Get It Back*, edited by Tom G. Palmer. Ottawa, IL: Jameson Books.

Palmer, Tom G. 2014. "The Political Economy of Empire and War." In *Peace, War, and Liberty*, edited by Tom G. Palmer, 62–82. Ottawa, IL: Jameson Books.

Parks, Tim. 2005. *Medici Money: Banking, Metaphysics, and Art in Fifteenth-Century Florence.* New York: W. W. Norton.

Pearson, Karl. (1892) 1990. *The Grammar of Science.* London: Black.

Pearson, Karl, and Margaret Moul. 1925. "The Problem of Alien Immigration into Great Britain, Illustrated by an Examination of Polish and Jewish Children." *Annals of Eugenics* 1 (2): 125–26.

Peterson, Christopher, and Martin E. P. Seligman, eds. 2004. *Character Strengths and Virtues: A Handbook and Classification.* Oxford: Oxford University Press.

Pink, Daniel H. 2012. *To Sell Is Human: The Surprising Truth about Moving Others.* New York: Riverhead Books.

Plantinga, Alvin. 2000. *Warranted Christian Belief.* New York: Oxford University Press.

Pomeranz, Kenneth. 2000. *The Great Divergence: China, Europe, and the Making of the Modern World Economy.* Princeton, NJ: Princeton University Press.

Reckendrees, A. 2015 . "Weimar Germany: The First Open Access Order That Failed?" *Constitutional Political Economy* 26 (1): 38–60.

Ringmar, Erik. 2007. *Why Europe Was First: Social Change and Economic Growth in Europe and East Asia 1500–2050.* London: Anthem.

Robertson, Dennis H. 1956. "What Does the Economist Economize?" In *Economic Commentaries.* London: Staples Press.

Rorty, Amélie Oksenberg. 1983. "Experiments in Philosophical Genre: Descartes' *Meditations.*" *Critical Inquiry* 9 (March): 545–65.

Rubin, Jared. 2017. *Rulers, Religion, and Riches: Why the West Got Rich and the Middle East Did Not.* Cambridge: Cambridge University Press.

Rumbold, Richard. 1685 (1961). "Speech from the Scaffold." In *The Levellers and the English Revolution*, by Henry Noel Brailsford. Stanford, CA: Stanford University Press.

Searle, John R. 2010. *Making the Social World: The Structure of Human Civilization.* Oxford: Oxford University Press.

Segrè, Gino, and Bettina Hoerlin. 2016. *The Pope of Physics: Enrico Fermi and the Birth of the Atomic Age.* New York: Henry Holt.

Sewell, William H. 1994. *The Rhetoric of Bourgeois Revolution: The Abbé Sieyes and What Is the Third Estate?* Durham, NC: University of North Carolina Press.

Smith, Adam. (1762–1763) 1978. *Lectures on Jurisprudence.* Edited by R. L. Meek, D. D. Raphael, and P. G. Stein. Oxford: Oxford University Press.

Smith, Adam. (1776) 1981. *An Inquiry into the Nature and Causes of the Wealth of Nations.* Edited by R. H. Campbell, A. S. Skinner, and W. B. Todd, 2 vols. Indianapolis, IN: Liberty Classics.

Smith, Monica L. 1999. "The Role of Ordinary Goods in Premodern Exchange." *Journal of Archaeological Method and Theory* 6:109–35.

Smith, Vernon L. 2008. *Rationality in Economics: Constructivist and Ecological Forms.* New York: Cambridge University Press.

Smith, Vernon and Bart J. Wilson. 2019. *Humanomics: Moral Sentiments and the Wealth of Nations for the Twenty-First Century.* Cambridge: Cambridge University Press.

Sprat, Thomas. (1667) 1958. *The History of the Royal Society.* Edited by J. Cope and H. Jones. St. Louis, MO: Washington University Studies.

Stevens, Wallace. 1934. "The Idea of Order at Key West." Poetry Foundation. https://www.poetryfoundation.org/poems/43431/the-idea-of-order-at-key-west.

Stigler, George J. 1961. "The Economics of Information." *Journal of Political Economy* 69:213–25. Reprinted in *The Organization of Industry*, 213–25. Homewood. IL: Irwin, 1968.

Storr, Virgil. 2012. *Understanding the Culture of Markets.* London: Routledge.

Sutch, Richard. 1991. "All Things Reconsidered: The Life-Cycle Perspective and the Third Task of Economic History." *Journal of Economic History* 51:271–88.

Taylor, Charles. 1989. *Sources of the Self: The Making of the Modern Identity.* Cambridge, MA: Harvard University Press.

Taylor, Charles. 2007. *A Secular Age.* Cambridge, MA: Harvard University Press.

Thomson, Erik. 2005. "Swedish Variations on Dutch Commercial Institutions, 1605–1655." *Scandinavian Studies* 77:331–46.

Tirole, Jean. 2006. *The Theory of Corporate Finance.* Princeton, NJ: Princeton University Press.

Tocqueville, Alexis de. 1856 (1955). *The Old Regime and the French Revolution.* New York: Anchor Books.

Viner, Jacob. (1950) 1991. "A Modest Proposal for Some Stress on Scholarship in Graduate Training." In *Jacob Viner: Essays on the Intellectual History of Economics*, edited by Douglas A. Irwin, 385–86. Princeton, NJ: Princeton University Press.

Wallis, John Joseph, and Douglass North. 1986. "Measuring the Transaction Sector in the American Economy, 1870–1970." In *Long-Term Factors in American Economic Growth*, edited by S. L. Engerman and R. E. Gallman, 95–161. Chicago: University of Chicago Press.

Walls, Laura Dassow. 2017. *Henry David Thoreau: A Life.* Chicago: University of Chicago Press.

Walras, Léon. (1874) 1954. *Elements of Pure Economics*. Translated by William Jaffé. Homewood, IL: Irwin.

Wasserstein, Ronald L., and Nicloe A. Lazar. 2016. "The ASA Statement on *p*-Values: Context, Process, and Purpose." *American Statistician* 70 (2): 129–33. http://amstat.tandfonline.com/doi/pdf/10.1080/00031305.2016.1154108.

Whaples, Robert. 2010. "Is Economic History a Neglected Field of Study?" and "Rejoinder," in *Historically Speaking* 11 (2): 17–20, 27.

White, James. B. 1984. *When Words Lose Their Meaning: Constitutions and Reconstitutions of Language, Character, and Community*. Chicago: University of Chicago Press.

Williamson, Jeffrey G. 1974. *Late Nineteenth-Century American Development: A General Equilibrium History*. Cambridge: Cambridge University Press.

Wilson, E. O. 1997. "Karl Marx Was Right, Socialism Works." Interview, Harvard University, March 27. http://www.froes.dds.nl/WILSON.htm.

Yeager, Leland B. 1999. "Should Austrians Scorn General Equilibrium Theory?" *Review of Austrian Economics* 11:19–30.

Yeats, W. B. (1928) 1992. *The Poems*. Edited by D. Albright. London: Everyman.

Ziliak, Stephen, and Deirdre Nansen McCloskey. 2008. *The Cult of Statistical Significance: How the Standard Error Costs Us Jobs, Justice, and Lives*. Ann Arbor: University of Michigan Press.

Index